Talk to the Devil

Surviving Severe Depression

HOWARD FRANK

Talk to the Devil

Independently Published by Howard Frank

Edited by s/b Chris Mele | http://bettergetaneditor.com/

Cover Design by Kristina Conatser | Captured by KC Designs

ISBN: 9798857769928

<u>DEDICATION</u>

I would like to dedicate this book to my family and friends who have supported me through the years of struggle with this disease. I know it couldn't have been easy for them, and for that, I am forever grateful.

CONTENTS

A Fateful Day

I sat at my desk as a reporter for a daily newspaper one summer day. My cell phone, buried deep in my pocket, rang, competing with the conversations, keyboards click-clacks and scanner chatter in our newsroom.

"This is Detective So-and-So. Is this Howard Frank?"

It wasn't unusual, as a reporter, to get a call from the police. Maybe he wanted to ask about a story I wrote.

He said, "I'm doing an investigation involving Craig Erickson. Do you know him?"

Craig was not only my neighbor but a close friend. We relied on each other for advice, and I was his go-to guy for leftover beer after his parties. Craig was also our family doctor. A brilliant diagnostician with a low-key and naturally comforting manner. So much so that all our doc friends sent their families to him.

"Yes, I know him," I said.

The detective asked, "Was Craig facing any financial problems?"

"No," I said.

"Any other kinds of problems?"

"No," I answered.

"Did you speak with Craig today?"

"No."

"Well, you were the last person he called from his cellphone," the detective stated.

"Craig didn't call me today."

The detective read me a phone number. "Is that your number?"

It was my home phone.

"What's going on?" I asked.

The detective said he wasn't authorized to say.

"OK," I said to the detective. "I've answered some of your questions, and now I'd like you to answer some of mine. Is Craig OK?"

"No," he answered.

"Is he hurt?"

"Yes."

Probing some more, I questioned, "Did someone hurt him?"

"No."

"Did he hurt himself?"

"Yes."

"Is he alive?" I became more concerned.

Hesitantly the detective replied, "I don't know."

Pause. "Where is he?"

"They flew him to St. Luke's in Bethlehem." The detective's sympathetic, gentle tone betrayed his own agony in making the call.

I jumped into my car to head home. Craig and I spoke two or three times a week. He knew my schedule and always knew to call my cellphone. Not today though. Why?

I tried rationalizing the conversation I had with the detective, desperately searching for alternative explanations for what I feared. There was a reason Craig called me at my home, which had an answering machine. He knew I wouldn't be there.

The machine sat in a small study next to a chair. I hit the play button. The first message was someone else. Second message inconsequential. Then the third began to play.

"Hi Howard, it's Craig," the message began, in his typical upbeat style. His greetings were always the same. I felt a moment of relief. It didn't last long.

"I've decided to end my life."

He continued to describe, first in that same calm voice, his financial concerns.

"I made some bad decisions," he said. "My credit is in the tank. The practice isn't doing well." The calm voice melted away.

In the space of a few sentences, it spiraled from the logical, friendly familiar voice to one of tormented grief. Apparently, he was a deeply tortured soul who had never revealed anything like it—to me or anyone else, as I learned over the following days.

He had been having financial problems. It wasn't as serious as he believed it to be. But that's the nature of depression. It distorts reality.

Craig was filled with guilt for what he was about to do, and wanted his family to know he loved them. He sobbed uncontrollably. The message lasted three minutes. The 21st century version of a suicide note.

Craig used a handgun he had stashed from his days in the military, retrieving it from a safe deposit box. He drove back to his office and shot himself in the parking lot. Right in front of his staff.

Craig was 36.

I realized what he'd done when I first played that phone message. I had this overwhelming urge to literally reach into that phone, back in time, just a few minutes, and get him back on the line. I wanted just one chance to talk to him, being his voice of reason, convincing him not to do it.

The pain for his parents, brother, our group of friends and, of course, his wife was beyond description. Anguish unlike any I'd ever seen.

The experience of losing someone to suicide is impossibly heartbreaking. Craig's parents were devastated, obviously never to be the same. It shakes the notion that things happen for a reason. It leaves friends wondering why and what we could have done to change things. And to understand that even doctors can become ill.

Craig's decision wasn't strategic. It wasn't a way to help his family financially through insurance. In fact, in the message, he mentioned that he didn't know if his life insurance would pay out for a self-inflicted death.

I believe Craig did it to escape a pain he could no longer tolerate. Imagine a pain that causes a person to overcome the basic instinct to survive. That's what Craig faced.

Craig and I had many discussions regarding suicide. I'd been concerned about a friend and Craig offered help. I will forever be haunted by those conversations and why he never mentioned anything to me about his own state of mind. Maybe it was the stigma that accompanies mental illness.

Craig was a true caregiver. He'd organize annual block parties and offered courtesy flu vaccinations to everyone one year.

Craig's death was a valuable lesson for me though. The loss of someone through suicide is different than other deaths. It feels so avoidable. So unnecessary. It taught me that the immeasurable anguish it leaves survivors with could never be worth the escape of my own pain.

Whenever I'd think about suicide, I'd think about my son, then a teenager, and what it would do to him. How it would destroy him for the rest of his life. I just couldn't do it. Craig's act has kept me from ending my own life. It's an irony that's never escaped me.

––––––––––––––

If you are having thoughts of suicide, call the National Suicide Prevention Lifeline at 1-800-273-8255 (TALK). You can find a list of additional resources at SpeakingOfSuicide.com/resources.

MY STORY

Witnessing Craig's tragic suicide shattered the fragile pieces of my own existence, and in an unexpected twist, it became a haunting catalyst that may have saved my very life.

The weight of depression has always been my relentless companion, a suffocating darkness that casts a long shadow over my professional endeavors and social connections. As I grew into adulthood, its insidious grip tightened, becoming an impenetrable barrier that thwarted my pursuit of happiness. I navigate this world as a functional depressive, fulfilling the roles of work, family, and home, yet the flicker of true joy eludes me, fading into the recesses of a distant memory. Despite traversing an arduous landscape of countless talk therapies, chemical treatments, and invasive interventions, the relief I yearn for remains elusive. Still, I refuse to surrender. With unwavering determination, I relentlessly pursue the latest therapies suggested by my doctors, clinging to the hope that someday the clouds will part and reveal a glimmer of respite.

But in this battle, I am acutely aware of the heavy burden of stigma, discrimination, and the judgment that society hurls upon those grappling with mental illness. It is a constant weight upon my shoulders, a perpetual fear of how others will perceive and treat me should I emerge from the shadows. Society, with its limited understanding, often perceives depression as a flaw of character, a sign of weakness rather than the insidious disease that it truly is.

The path of mental illness is a treacherous one, fraught with countless graduations from one level of therapy to another, each step plunging deeper into the abyss. With each escalation, my self-image diminishes, eroded by the relentless onslaught of despair. But within this narrative lies a story of survival, a testament to the resilience that dwells within me. It is a chronicle of confronting life's adversities head-on, even in the face of desperate sorrow, and discovering the inner fortitude to persevere through the darkest of moments. Some of the experiences that unfolded were surreal, their intensity matched only by the futility of my persistence.

In sharing these experiences and reflections, I find solace in the tales of others who have walked a similar path. It is in these shared narratives that I discover solace, a reassurance that I am not alone in this bewildering journey. These offer glimpses of understanding, helping me unravel the intricate threads of my own condition and providing a glimmer of hope in the face of the unknown.

EVOLUTION

Early Memories

The darkness started to shroud me when I was a little boy. My mother noticed it when I was about five. We were in public somewhere. It was about to rain, and I became melancholy for no particular reason. She reached into her purse and withdrew a clenched fist.

"I'm going to give you some happy pills," she said. Then my mother moved her hand toward my mouth and told me to open up. She stuck something on my tongue. I couldn't feel it but followed her directions and swallowed.

"Happy pills!" I can clearly remember saying or thinking with a smile.

I couldn't sense the pills, but I remember imagining they were probably small and thin like pistachio seeds. She'd do that whenever she noticed my sadness.

The pills, of course, were imaginary, but since every mom is part homemaker, disciplinarian, and physician, she intrinsically knew the value of a placebo.

Later, in my late 30s, and weeks before she died, I came clean. I told her I had been treated for depression over several years.

She came clean herself. She said she wanted to get me help as a child, but my father was resistant, just as many fathers would be during the 1960s before mental illness lost some of its shame. It was in that conversation, one of the last I had with her, that I realized I had probably been depressed all my life.

The pistachio seeds came back to me.

It would take me a long time to seek out treatment in my early adulthood and not always at my own choosing. But that's the way I have found the entire process: a series of escalations, confrontations, and thresholds. Moving up from one level of treatment to the next, each one a difficult surrender of ourselves.

I've been diagnosed with major, treatment-resistant depression. I've been through many therapies and tried countless drugs. Though I've stabilized through a cocktail of medications, I'm still searching for relief.

No pain I know can be measured on the same scale as the agony of severe depression. It wraps you with its tentacles of negative thoughts and emotions and won't let you go.

This story includes my observations and research of the disease, the treatment process, and most of all, my effort to survive. One commonality those who are depressed share is the frustration of not being able to describe the pain and make those around them understand it. I am going to take a shot at bridging that gap.

I will try to characterize it in my own way and hope those close to someone suffering will understand their loved ones better. If you're afflicted, you might find comfort in knowing you're not alone in your suffering.

ADOLESCENT ANGST

I grew up in Queens, New York, a suburb of Manhattan, as I liked to think. Two parents, one brother, middle class and no life-shattering experiences that a soft-talking therapist would uncover down the line. But I was always emotional. I'd cry easily. I had a temper and would get frustrated, while lacking the skills to deal with that frustration.

We lived in a development of garden apartments — two- and three-bedroom configurations—for military veterans. The two-story brick buildings had small gardens in front tended by the upstairs and downstairs residents. There were four apartments at each entrance. It was white, mostly Jewish, and for the most part, crime-free.

Our apartment was a two-bedroom—one for my parents and one for my brother and me to share. He was a year older than me.

We had bunk beds to make the room work and always fought to get the preferred top bed.

When I was about 8 years old, my grandfather moved in with us. He was getting on—in his late 70s by then I'd guess, and after a broken arm, could no longer live by himself.

My grandfather had a crooked smile. When he was younger, he had intentionally punctured his eardrum to avoid having to join the Russian Army in World War I. The right side of his mouth drooped, giving him a permanently grouchy look.

My brother and I shared our bedroom with our grandfather. My parents moved some things around and put a single bed at a right angle to the bunk beds. The room couldn't have been bigger than 12 feet by 10 feet.

But my brother and I welcomed our grandfather. In the end, what grandparents aren't special? We never thought of it as an imposition. It just seemed natural to us. We weren't teenagers yet when it might have made a bigger difference. But we loved him, and he was a member of the family.

The arrangement lasted about five years, until my grandfather required more individualized attention. He moved to a nursing home on Long Island that my uncle managed, and we went to visit him every Saturday. We'd take him to Nathan's restaurant—they had an enormous one there. My father would dump a handful of change on the table for my brother and me to buy hot dogs and fries at the counters.

One day when I was about 13, I returned home from a Little League game. My grandfather had been in the hospital, but I didn't know or think much about it. I knocked on the front door of the apartment and my parents were standing in the doorway.

"Grandpa died," my father said.

I was inconsolable. It was the first loss I had to deal with. And after living together all those years, I had grown close to him. My brother handled the news by going out to play stickball. We were quite different.

SCHOOLING

I attended New York City public schools. When I began junior high school, seventh through ninth grades, the school offered to put me in a two-year program, essentially skipping a grade. My parents opted out. They obviously didn't think I had the emotional maturity or was too fragile to deal with it. How right they were.

I had my share of identity-seeking strife, probably no different than others my age. I went to a high school with thousands of students, and it was easy to get lost in the crowd. *Except for me.*

During adolescence, my complexion was a mess. I was self-conscious, which made me more introverted and bluer. There were days when my face was so broken out, I would skip school. I suppose the stubborn acne triggered my then-unidentified battle with depression.

But I remember one girl who showed interest in me despite my spotted face. She even waited for me after school one day to ride the bus home together. We lived close to each other. After all these years, I can still remember that insignificant event. We became friends—I didn't know how to become anything else with a girl anyway.

ANGER AND DEPRESSION

When I turned 16, I landed a job at a local McDonald's. The other employees at the restaurant were about the same age since it was a bottom-of-the-barrel entry-level job.

I made lots of friends and began partying with them during our free time. We'd hang out in the restaurant's parking lot, listening to Led Zeppelin, The Who and Deep Purple on 8-track tapes. It was an evening destination.

I met a girl there about a year older than me. Lisa had long dark hair, a cute, upturned nose, and freckles. We began dating. Our dating became serious, and we were immediately mutually exclusive. Not like I had other options at the time. I was an inexperienced, shy teen with bad skin.

I dated Lisa during my last year of high school and all through college. We were extremely close. It was my first real relationship and it brought me joy. It lasted until grad school. But there were times when I felt anger and may have come close to aggressive behavior with her.

I have never hit my wife or anyone else, although my wife has poked me in anger with a powerful finger from time to time.

Anger isn't a cataloged core symptom of depression in the Diagnostic and Statistical Manual of Mental Disorders (DSMMD), the industry bible, but irritability is. For me, it was a lack of coping skills conflicting with my perfectionist tendencies and the value of fairness. I couldn't deal well with shortcomings in either area. In fact, there is a strong link between irritability and depression.

I still fight those urges from time to time. Matured and schooled in behavior management, I've learned to walk away from the dinner table or conversation when those feelings crop up. My wife says walking away is a childish form of behavior. For me, it's a coping mechanism.

HIGHER EDUCATION

College at a state university in New York began as one big party. That is, until I decided to get serious during my second year. It gave me enough time to raise my GPA from those disastrous early grades. I had been floating in a world of uncertainty, not knowing where I was going career-wise.

Roommate problems plagued my first semester. I was the third man out, the straightest of the three. I'd walk home from class feeling anxious and melancholy, searching for ways to escape the situation. It triggered my depression. I spoke up to the residential supervisor and was eventually paired with a new roommate. No more housing issues from then on. The depression eased.

I found an interest in a subspecialty of psychology called human factor engineering, also known as ergonomics—designing systems and hardware that matched human anatomy and behaviors. None of that counseling or abnormal psychology for me. I was methodical and analytical and didn't like warm and fuzzy stuff. Why not grad school for ergonomics?

During my senior year of college, I met an economics professor who earned an MBA from the University of Michigan in Ann Arbor. He was planning to go back there to get his Ph.D. in business and convinced me to apply to business schools.

It was my family tradition. My father was a controller, my mother was a bookkeeper, and my brother became a CPA. Business was a natural progression. I applied to several schools, including Michigan, which accepted me. I had to choose between it and New York University. Michigan, a top-rated program, seemed like the obvious choice.

Those were happy days for me. The end of a college career and a future with the best and brightest. All was well except for graduation itself. My eye was infected, and I ducked as many classmates as I could. I remember sitting, depressed, with a sympathetic female friend at graduation, who eventually came out to me years later. Who knew?

GLARING SIGNS

Graduate school was the first time I became acutely aware of my depression. I was a first-semester MBA student at Michigan. The campus was magnificent, filled with the old-world charm of buildings that stood for more than 100 years, along with the occasional modern structure of a well-funded school.

I was a social science major as an undergrad and didn't have any background in the business curriculum that was now giving me fits. My first two tests, in accounting and statistics, were failing grades. I questioned how I was going to make it through the program.

My anxiety was suffocating. There was the pressure to keep up with these gifted students and master an entirely new area of study. I carried a constant feeling of hopelessness. I was lost. I wanted a way out. But there weren't any good choices. I couldn't drop out—that would be a disappointment to me, my family, and friends—and just wasn't an option. I couldn't admit defeat. Plus, I had those school loans an MBA from Michigan would help repay. It seemed like I had to go on.

Then it came to me. It came to me while walking home one day from class to my off-campus house. I thought, if I got hit by a car and injured, I would be able to gracefully take time off from the program. It was a way out. I remember constantly hoping I'd get hit by a car.

I didn't though and toughed it out. My grades improved as I swallowed my sadness and self-doubt and worked through the program. It didn't help that my entry grades and standardized test scores put me at the bottom of my class. Insecurity reigned. But I trudged through.

Job interviews were another area where my depression seeped out. Recruiters came to the school to interview for summer internships and post-degree jobs. Looking back, I realized my demeanor reflected a sad, downtrodden attitude. Employers were looking for upbeat people. I was the opposite.

I received some second interviews and was even flown around the country to visit prospective employers. But no good offers ensued. I'm sure, looking back, it was my deep-seated gloominess rearing its ugly head that made me a bad bet for an employer.

The Real World

Yet, I persevered. My first job in advertising in New York City wasn't fun. It wasn't a good fit. Again, my depression projected a negative attitude, something deeply frowned upon in the client-centric advertising industry.

Then I hit my stride. I found a marketing job in the fashion industry, something which still makes me laugh. It was with Sasson, a designer jeans company that was big at the time, in the early '80s, along with Calvin Klein, Gloria Vanderbilt, and Jordache. Money flowed into the company, which was owned by a charismatic young French Tunisian, and I was a part of something good.

I began, of course, as a junior member of the team, and spent an inordinate amount of time at the copy machine. That's where I met my future wife, a designer who was also on the corporate ladder's bottom rung. She used a teletype machine in the copy room. That was long before email.

Teresa was a tall Texan with blonde hair and blue eyes, something foreign to a New York Jew, and we took to each other. We were among the few non-partiers in the company, where, in those days, you could frequently find people snorting cocaine in bathroom stalls. I thought naively for the longest time they had colds. We decided to live together after a couple of years.

I climbed the corporate ladder and after a few years became the director of marketing. But the Tunisian's money attracted a lot of people and the company's owner got in with a bad crowd. My boss began dealing with racketeers and got hooked on drugs and booze. Over my last couple of years at the company, he held meetings in his Upper East Side townhouse, complete with indoor swimming pool and elevator. Used tissues and liquor bottles littered his bed and the surrounding area.

The Tunisian became paranoid, thinking his younger brother was trying to kill him. I walked into his bedroom one evening to deliver papers. Men with compact automatic weapons lined the walls of the room. I knew it was time to get out.

LICENSING

I accepted a position as a partner in an up-and-coming licensing company about to do an IPO, an initial public offering of stock. It was a risky move for me but provided the promise of substantial financial rewards.

Still, my depression was growing. I lacked patience and instigated frequent arguments about nothing in particular with Teresa in the streets of Manhattan, oblivious to the place or appropriateness of the conversation. The triggers were so trivial that I can't remember these anymore. Yet I'd argue with her. My productivity at work suffered because of my undeveloped coping skills.

It was the late '80s and I'd been having problems with my anger and moods. I insisted I didn't need help but as time passed, my symptoms became worse. My moods swung lower, and Teresa became the focus of my hostility.

FIRST ATTEMPTS FOR HELP

Teresa and I were lounging on top of our building, a 100-plus-year-old restored brownstone on West 88th Street in Manhattan. I was in my late 20s. The building had a roof garden seemingly transported from Better Homes and Gardens. That was my wife, a sweater designer and creator of knits, knacks and nature. She never stopped making everything she touched beautiful.

But the tranquil surroundings stood in stark contrast to the atmosphere of our conversation. She was done. Fed up with my crankiness and incessant anger, she gave me an ultimatum: Get help or she would leave. *It was no threat.*

A few years earlier, she'd attended a professional women's networking gathering. One of the women who spoke was a psychologist based in the Financial District. The psychologist specialized in helping professionals navigate their way through mental illness and the stress of the business world. My girlfriend offered to make an appointment. I reluctantly said yes.

That was a big step. Up until then, I was just a normal guy, yeah, maybe a bit moody but nothing I couldn't handle. But once I made the appointment, I was no longer that person. I became a person who was in psychological counseling. It was a big self-perception difference.

After several sessions, the therapist, a no-nonsense professional who seemed to understand the business world psyche, told me I was too depressed for her to work with. I had to see a psychiatrist and get some meds before her treatments would be effective.

I resisted seeing a psychiatrist for a few weeks. I didn't want to go there. But with my mood sinking every day, I eventually gave in. I became a patient of a psychiatrist, taking antidepressants. I'd received another label for my mental illness. It was a club I never conceived I'd join.

This was a recurring pattern during my treatment: Needing greater intervention, more meds, and different therapies. I resisted each, as every stop redefined who I was. First someone in therapy. Then a psychiatric patient. Then someone on antidepressants. Every change was like a step on a ladder, each one met with defiance and each one lowering my self-image.

TALK THERAPY

My first exposure to mental health treatment was that pragmatic, serious-minded psychologist with an office in the shadows of the former World Trade Center.

I would take the subway to her offices from work every week, passing through the expansive, multi-story atrium that served as one of the tower's lobbies.

The psychologist was direct, practical, and demanding. If I didn't feel like talking one day, she'd turn that right around on me. She'd remind me it wouldn't do me much good to stay silent.

I was struggling at work, trying to keep a brave face but walking around looking sad.

She asked me, "Who is your favorite actor?"

I said, "James Woods."

He was a quirky actor who is probably best known for his role as Sharon Stone's junkie boyfriend in Martin Scorsese's film, *Casino*.

She told me to pretend to be James Woods—*act* when with my peers. Perform like you're upbeat and happy. Fake it 'til you make it.

It was a survival-in-the-jungle type of strategy. It wasn't good to mope around an office that was trying to accomplish positive results. Especially as a manager, since your behavior would affect those reporting to you.

I followed her advice and even felt better doing so. Positive behavior led to positive thoughts and emotions.

It was a part of an area of psychological therapy known as cognitive-behavioral psychology. It's the idea that thoughts, emotions, and behavior form a triangle, each affecting the other. Sometimes you can change your behavior by changing your thought process, which leads to more positive emotions. Also, by acting in a more positive way, you can change your emotional state and thus your cognitive perspective.

The strategy helped me through a tumultuous time later on with a toxic newspaper editor. I began having some control over my behavior and subsequent thoughts and emotions. But it wasn't enough to overcome the inexplicable tidal wave of depression that would wash over me later in life.

MONEY DIDN'T BRING HAPPINESS

The licensing company was quite a ride. Both my partner and I came from mainstream fashion labels with licensing businesses.

The idea was to create a new brand, called NO EXCUSES, and sign-up manufacturers to produce NO EXCUSES branded goods in 30 or so product categories. These ranged from jeans to sportswear, accessories, and footwear.

We would pool their advertising money, coordinate marketing campaigns, and collect royalties from their sales. It was a successful strategy for both our former employers.

My partner was smart and a risk-taker. He had signed several licensees in different product categories simply based on his reputation and persuasiveness. But when I brought in a blue jean maker, I knew from Sasson, the business took off.

It was the height of the acid-wash craze, and we were right in the middle of it, selling as many jeans as we could make. We even did a scandalous commercial featuring Donna Rice, the newly discovered girlfriend of then-married Democratic presidential candidate Gary Hart. The media portrayed Rice as a Jezebel, homewrecker, and political career destroyer.

Donna Rice was a stunning blonde with all-American good looks. The 15-second commercial mocked her refusal to explain her behavior with Hart publicly. Two versions of the commercial were shot. In both, she lounged horizontally on chaise, decked out in NO EXCUSES jeans and denim jacket. Slinky saxophone music played as the camera panned from her feet, across her legs and to her face.

Her lines were simple: "I make no excuses. I only wear them," and "Fifteen seconds? Not enough time." Our company was building a bad-boy reputation.

The publicity from the commercials alone got us geometrically more media coverage than our modest television buy. Our hire of Donna Rice made the front pages of the New York Post and the New York Daily News, grand slams in the public relations business. My partner and I were, for the time being, considered stars and marketing geniuses, although the idea came from my partner and our marketing director.

At the same time, we were working with a Wall Street underwriter to offer shares of our company to the public. Since my partner and I owned most of the shares, we would benefit from the IPO.

We went public in the late '80s, and the share price quickly multiplied, pumped by brokers who earned commissions from stock sales. Even though our company was more of a concept than a profitable entity, investors jumped in. We raised several million dollars, a lot of money at the time for what we were working with. The office was jubilant.

One of my partner's friends came into my office, smiling widely and patting me on the back.

"You're a millionaire," he said. "A multi-millionaire!"

It hadn't really hit me, and besides, it was all on paper. As principals, we couldn't sell our stock for two years. By that time, the prices would sink. But it felt good for a while.

Still, I had my issues. I never shook that pervasive sadness, even at the thought of riches. It convinced me that my depression went beyond my circumstances, deeper into my psyche.

The Park Incident

It was a hot day in June during the 1980s, with the temperatures reaching nearly 90 degrees. Teresa and I ran in Central Park after work almost every day, along with many others. We'd enter the park at 90th Street and Fifth Avenue and do a four- or six-mile loop.

At that time, the park closed to vehicle traffic at 7 p.m. A road wound lazily in an oval through the rectangular park, and runners generally followed a counterclockwise route. The road was divided into two sections, with a runner's lane on the left-hand side, the interior of the loop. Bicyclists used the two vehicle lanes to its right. There was an orderly madness to it all, but it worked.

We jogged our way north toward our turn, a cut-through at about 100th Street. That cutoff would later become infamous as the site of the attack on the Central Park jogger. But there were plenty of people around that evening, and daylight added to our comfort.

As we approached the cut-off, I heard shouting behind me. I turned, looked over my left shoulder, and saw one of those three-wheeled police vehicles that they used to get around the congested city, coming up right behind us. I pulled Teresa, running to my left, across my body, and to my right. The vehicle, driving in the congested runner's lanes, just missed hitting her and continued for a few yards.

Teresa spun 360 degrees, ending up facing in the direction of our travel and that of the vehicle. She raised her hand in anger, and from a clenched fist, her middle finger shot up.

I could see the officer's bloodshot eyes in his mirror through the centered back window of the vehicle. He saw Teresa give him the finger, immediately stopped the vehicle, and exited through its door on its left.

He came charging after Teresa, armed with his nightstick, and said, "She called me a black bastard."

Uh-oh. Teresa said no such thing, nor was it in her Texas vocabulary. But I could tell this officer had a chip on his shoulder and was pissed. I knew we were in trouble.

We later learned the officer's name was Flowers.

Flowers grabbed Teresa and called for backup. A large group of runners and bikers circled us, yelling at him for plowing through the runner's lane.

Two other officers arrived quickly, and as I pleaded for them to let her go, the officers held me, with their backs to Flowers. He fumbled with Teresa's hands, trying to handcuff her, and hit her in the right eye with his nightstick.

"He hit me. He hit me," I clearly remember her saying in disbelief. Her face would sport a bruise from it for a couple of weeks.

Flowers put her in the back seat of the backup police car, and the other officers drove her to the Central Park precinct. Flowers followed with his three-wheeled buggy, and I had to run a couple of miles to get to the station on my own.

I was dripping with sweat when I arrived, having run faster than my normal pace. It was a long two miles. I leaned over the desk officer's counter, pleading for his attention and my case. My sweat dripped onto his oversized and aged logbook spread out on the counter.

All he would say was, "I wasn't there."

In the meantime, Flowers had taken Teresa, with her hands handcuffed behind her back, into a private room at the station. Since it was hot that evening, she wore a thin t-shirt and short shorts, which were popular with runners in those days. Suddenly, alone with the officer, she felt terribly exposed.

Flowers berated her, raging he was a police officer and she had to respect him. Another man heard the commotion and entered the room. He was older, and as it turned out, the chief of detectives for the precinct. He would later receive notoriety for his leadership during the Central Park jogger's case.

The chief admonished Flowers for being alone in the room with Teresa and kicked them out. When I arrived, she was standing in the lobby of the station, still handcuffed, trying to suppress her tears.

Flowers searched through a thick book to figure out what to charge Teresa with. He gave her a summons for disorderly conduct and one to me for harassment. We left as soon as we could. Now we'd have to hire an attorney and go to court.

The next evening, I went back to the spot in the park where the incident occurred in hopes of finding witnesses. As luck would have it, two people, a runner, and biker, saw me standing on the side of the road and stopped to talk. They both agreed to serve as witnesses for us, and we exchanged information.

Ironically, as I walked back to Teresa's East Side apartment, I passed a parked police car. To my surprise, Flowers was sitting in there, eating his dinner. We looked at each other in disbelief, and he just shrugged his shoulders, as if to say, it happened and I'm sorry.

Teresa and I were worried sick about going to court and being accused of a crime. We were runners, not criminals, and we were out of our element.

An attorney joined us for our first court appearance in downtown Manhattan, where the state and federal courthouses are located. About eight or 10 other suspects cited by Flowers were there too. Apparently, the court grouped an officer's cases for appearances to make best use of the officer's time.

Flowers didn't show up. The judge rescheduled the appearance. All our anxiety was for naught, and we'd have to go through it again.

Flowers failed to show up for the second scheduled appearance a few weeks later. The judge wanted to give him another chance and set a new date. Again, our fears rose and fell, and our desire to get it over with would have to wait.

Flowers didn't show up for the third appearance. This time, the judge dismissed the charges against us and all of Flowers' other suspects. I looked at our attorney, confused about what was happening. He motioned for us to quickly leave the courtroom. I glanced at the judge, who, seeing my confusion, gave me a warm smile of reassurance. The monkey was off our back.

During this process, which took place over several months, we learned we could file a complaint against Flowers. I was still angry for what he put us through and began the necessary steps. We filed a complaint with the city's Civilian Complaint Review Board, a sanctioned group of non-police investigators and attorneys. A judge would hear the case and had the power to impose civil penalties.

Flowers got an attorney to defend himself, and the lawyer launched a public relations campaign to destroy our credibility. He told the New York Daily News that Teresa and I were drug dealers out to get him. The story, without our names, appeared in the paper. Flowers was referred to as a hero cop for his fight against illegal drugs. We would later learn of the irony of that claim.

One evening at the entrance to our apartment building on West 70th Street, Teresa and I noticed a baggie that looked to contain white powder on the ground. I kicked it with my toe, amusedly suspicious of what it was. We stepped over it and walked on. Afterwards, we agreed it might have been an attempt by Flowers to catch us with cocaine and undermine our case. Again, we'd later learn how likely this was.

Although amused by the apparent cocaine and our suspicions of its origins, we got scared. Having witnessed Flower's rage, we were worried he'd pursue us. So, we contacted the attorneys prosecuting the case against the officer and told them we were out. They balked and asked to come and meet with us at our apartment.

The prosecutors came over one evening, and we had what we now refer to as "cop cookies" waiting for them. We told them what happened with the baggie and our worries, yet they convinced us to proceed with the case. The trial again was held downtown. Teresa and I would testify, along with the two witnesses. Flowers, I assume, testified as well.

Because of the media campaign Flowers' attorney orchestrated, the trial drew the attention of the local NBC affiliate's news department. I recognized the reporter from her daily appearances on TV.

We were kept in a room during the trial so as not to be exposed to other testimony. When I was asked to enter the imposing courtroom to testify, I noticed a woman sitting on my left in the back, looking at me through something. I walked over to her during a break, and saw she was sketching us for the news, using a small pair of binoculars to see us up close. I'd later learn the judge, not used to so much attention, had asked her for the sketch as a memento when she was done with it.

I sat in a witness chair slightly off center to the right of the courtroom. The judge's bench blocked my view of the left side of the courtroom, where Flowers sat at the defense table. I looked around the corner of that table before I began and saw Flowers giving me a death stare. The fear it stirred is still seared into my brain.

The two prosecutors sat directly in front of me. They asked me to describe the sequence of events and handed it over to the defense. That got testy. At one point I was asked to leave the room, and thanks to that reporter, I'd later learn why.

The aggressive defense continued questioning my recall of the events. The park incident happened, so recounting it was no big deal. Then the defense attorney, closing his questioning, hit me with the *got ya* question.

"Mr. Frank, isn't it true that you care so much about Ms. Hicks that you would do anything for her?"

It was obvious where he was going, so I said, "It's true, if someone attacked Teresa again, I would try to protect her." I could see the prosecutor pump his fist in satisfaction and give me a big smile. I left the stand and returned to the waiting room.

Teresa went back to work after her testimony, but I stuck around to talk to the prosecutors. During a break, I bumped into the reporter in the hallway. She wanted to interview Teresa. Then the reporter told me that when I was asked to leave the room, the lawyers and judge were discussing whether certain questioning would be allowed. It concerned my interactions with Elton John, who Sasson Jeans sponsored during one of his tours. The information was considered hearsay, coming from a former police officer working for the company, and wasn't allowed. The attempt to tarnish my credibility failed.

Then she told me that testimony revealed Flowers, a Vietnam veteran, was known to shake down drug dealers on the Upper West Side and steal their drugs. That made him popular with the local shop owners, but also explained those blood-red eyes I saw when he was traversing the park that night, between his East Side patrol area and the Upper West Side. The implication was he was a cocaine user and was experiencing hyper-rage from the stimulant.

The lead prosecutor called us a few weeks later. The judge ruled Flowers had acted inappropriately and suspended him for a week without pay. Flowers quit the force shortly after the ruling. We never learned if he was forced out, but we had our suspicions.

The incident had a profound effect on my depression. I felt helpless throughout the ordeal and became deeply melancholy and unmotivated. My anxiety peaked with the experience and didn't let down even after its resolution. I ran less, feared what would happen to me on the streets, and my relationship with Teresa suffered. We fought about going after Flowers, and it opened a short-lasting chasm between us.

Now we look back at that incident 35 years earlier with a sense of astonishment, achievement, and disgust. It wrecked my digestive system at the time and made me generally angry. It also shook my confidence in a law enforcement system where police defend or ignore the bad acts of fellow police. It's not surprising that people who share a dangerous profession form a brotherhood. But it can't go so far as to perpetuate a wrong. And all these years later, it's still happening today.

FEARS LEAD TO SADNESS

There were happy times. Like when my career blossomed in my 20s. I made decent money, traveled extensively, and had a management position as the director of marketing for a hot jeans company. Things were good.

Teresa and I made an annual Memorial Day weekend trip to Austin, Texas, to visit her sister and brother. Both were attending the University of Texas. Her sister, Teresa and I would make an excursion to San Antonio during our visits, a 90-minute drive from Austin.

On the way to San Antonio, we'd stop at a little town called New Braunfels. The Guadalupe River passed through the town. It offered several launching sites where you could rent an inner tube with a plywood bottom and float down the narrow winding river.

The river's icy cold waters flowed from the Rockies, in stark contrast to the hot, humid weather we'd invariably get. The current was generally tame, and it wasn't unusual to see people rent an extra inner tube to carry their beer, or on more than one occasion, a dog.

Though the current was gentle, the river had a series of dams to control the water flow. The dams usually had a drop of four to six feet, where water rushed over the tops and crashed into the river below.

We tied our tubes together so we would float down the river as a group. The water snaked through the woods and the dams came without much warning.

We reached one such dam. I was at the back of our tethered inner tube train. The water was rough at the bottom, and as the other two tubes made their way over the dam, mine stalled at the bottom of the crashing water.

I landed on my back, face up, with the thunderous wash pinning my chest to the bottom of the river. I fought to get out, but the weight and force of the overflowing water was too strong for me. My head was submerged, though at moments I could fight to get a gasp of air. But that wasn't sustainable.

I was drowning. My first thought was not to panic and try to wiggle myself out. After a few futile seconds, I remember telling myself, *OK, it's time to panic.* I tried shouting for help when my mouth could reach the air. But I knew it was a lost cause.

I thought to myself, *What a way to die.* It was so ordinary, so random. Just having fun on a day off.

Events seemed to slow down around me but sped up in my head. Once my lungs filled with water, would I lose consciousness, or just continue to suffer oxygen hunger for a time?

Just at that moment, I felt someone tugging on my arm and leg. It was Teresa, pulling me sideways, out from under the falling water. We cleared the dam's rush and she anxiously paced in the thigh-deep water. I was fairly calm—it was probably the relief of not having drowned.

We finished the trek down the river in the tubes, untethered, and walked around the dams to avoid them from then on.

While Teresa was shaken by the experience, I didn't have much of a reaction. I don't think that was the depression or having a death wish. I just didn't want to drown. I was simply in shock. But when I got on a flight a day later, it hit me all at once. My limbs began shaking and I felt a sensation of dread as to what might have been.

Ever since then I've had an aversion—no—fear of water. I can go into a pool, but I don't enjoy it. That's a part of my depression since it's something I used to love. But swimming brings back memories of the immense power of water and its unforgiving nature. It's a trigger for me.

THE BIG BANG

It was the eve of Labor Day weekend. I was on my way to work at 6:20 a.m., on a Friday at the end of the summer. I looked forward to curling up with my New York Times, a muffin and coffee.

I walked down Sixth Avenue, and turned onto West 40th Street, where my NO EXCUSES office was. In the darkness, the flashing lights of a fire truck and ConEd utility vehicle caught my attention.

I ignored it. I wanted that muffin.

As time went by, another fire truck, more ConEd trucks and an ambulance arrived. I was preparing for a meeting on a clunky white Toshiba laptop, so I paid it little attention.

We had the good fortune to face Bryant Park, a nearly 10-acre grassy area with winding sidewalks and park benches. It was newly renovated and sat behind the enormous New York Public Library, between Fifth and Sixth Avenues. An oasis in the jungle.

Employees began wandering into the office and told me the police were closing the street. My small office had a floor-to-ceiling, wall-to-wall window. I'd sit with my back to it. I swiveled my chair around and could see other employees gather in the park. By this time, the streets were bright with sunshine.

As I stood at my desk shuffling papers, a powerful, concussive shudder shook the building. Instantly, I could hear glass breaking behind my back. A wave of air, much like an ocean wave, picked me up and carried me over the desk.

When I opened my eyes, I could see my feet next to a picture that was still hanging on the wall. I was upside down, with my head on top of a table pedestal. Its glass top shattered like the window from the explosion.

ConEd had been working underground that morning, dealing with an electrical problem.

The underbelly of New York City is rife with nasty objects, mostly garbage and the rotting corpses of dead rats. The decomposing bodies and decaying organic garbage released methane gas, which is highly flammable. A spark from a malfunctioning circuit ignited the gas and an explosion followed.

It obliterated my window and blew a 300-pound manhole cover 20 feet into the air, striking just above the window. Razor-sharp shards of pointed, heavy glass, some more than two feet long, surrounded me. My head and left hand were bleeding, but otherwise, I seemed fine.

Firefighters rushed up a set of stairs and pounded on the stairwell door, which as all New Yorkers know, was locked from the outside. They began taking an axe to it, until one of my office mates came to open it.

The first responders sized me up. My blood pressure was 200 over something. I was in shock, they said. A firefighter dabbed the blood and put me on a stretcher.

He stared at the oversized glass shards, looked at me, and said, "You're the luckiest person in New York City today."

They took me out of the building on that stretcher, in front of all my coworkers who were across the street in the park. Some were crying. They saw me blown off my feet and didn't know I was OK.

The medical crew left me on the stretcher for a few minutes behind an ambulance on Sixth Avenue. The street was packed with pedestrians, who were rubbernecking at the sight of the flashing lights. Some associates, jeans makers I believe, passed by and asked what happened. I explained what little I knew as I lay on my back, bandaged. It was turning into a comedy.

The ambulance, with suspension that was rendered useless many miles ago, took me to the hospital. It was the now closed St. Vincent's, known then as an AIDS hospital. In those days, AIDS was a death sentence.

I had a mild concussion with a few small cuts and was treated then released. The young attending physician looked like he had just woken up and wasn't too happy about having to treat me. I took a taxi back to Teresa's office to let her know I was OK.

Meanwhile, she heard the explosion from her office several blocks away and came to the scene to see if I was hurt. One of my coworkers told her what happened. This was before cellphones, but luckily, she called her office and found out I was there. My brother also called her office after not being able to reach me.

Word got around fast, and after all, it was a really loud boom.

The adrenaline had subsided, and I became aware of my body. Out of nowhere, my back began to hurt. I don't know if it was from the compression of my spine after landing on my head, or the twisting as I flew through the air, but it was the beginning of a long, painful journey that would bring with it unanticipated depression.

The back pain, which triggered more depression, was an unforeseen consequence of a random event that can define our lives if we let it.

In the aftermath, I had a long battle with ConEd. The utility refused to pay for the ambulance. It eventually gave me several thousand dollars for my injuries, but not without a fight. The company had no soul.

STIGMA

I stepped into my partner's office one day at NO EXCUSES. He was sitting with a consultant he'd become close to.

I mentioned I had to find a family doctor. My partner, whose father founded the Candie's shoe brand said, "It's funny, you have a psychiatrist, but not a doctor."

Both men got a good laugh over the remark, and I left the room.

I never talked about being treated by a psychiatrist and it was a mystery how he knew. But the cruelty and insensitivity of his comments and their reaction became a permanent reminder of the widespread attitude attached to mental illness, particularly in the workplace — and among educated people no less.

That's the belief of so many toward mental illness, even these days, almost 30 years later. It carries a taint that leads people to discriminate against and think less of those afflicted. There are many familiar misconceptions about mental illness. The most common is that mental illness is due to mental weakness. In fact, it's the opposite.

Some of the strongest people I know have a mental illness. That strength comes from the need to summon the courage to operate in the real world with this silent, painful disease. You develop resilience.

No one would make jokes about someone suffering from multiple sclerosis or Parkinson's disease. But with depression and mental illness, it's fair game, so you're compelled to keep it hidden.

Even my own brother made fun of me.

Shortly before my mother, a widow, had a fatal stroke, she told me he took $30,000 out of an account she had set up for him and me. She gave him signatory powers over the account. He needed money and was obviously desperate.

I told my brother about my treatment for depression shortly before I confronted him about the money. I felt bad for him and his money issues, and thought by telling him about my depression, it would level the playing field, each of us with our own secret problems. He denied the theft, saying our mother told him to take the money. He then went on to make fun of my illness, calling me "medication man."

To be honest, the stealing hurt more.

The family always trusted each other over money. We never had much, and we respected it. I was in shock when he denied stealing. My hurt and outrage triggered another period of deep depression. I was a wreck that he would betray our trust.

But looking back, he had always bullied me, as older brothers sometimes do. One time as a child, he pushed me off a table and dislocated my arm. He lacked empathy.

The stigma attached to depression guided my choice of mental health providers too. When it came time to choose a psychiatrist after moving to Pennsylvania, I went about 30 miles from my home for treatment. I didn't want to bump into anyone I knew at the practice, thus revealing my secret.

The stigma aggravated my depression, filling me with guilt, self-doubt and weakening my self-esteem. I, like so many others, internalized the stigma.

The most harmful aspect of the stigma is that it keeps those suffering from seeking treatment. I know it did in my case, as I put off seeing a therapist for some time. It also kept me from trying more aggressive therapies in a timelier manner. The disgrace attached to mental illness leads to greater and prolonged suffering.

Society may be changing as we become more educated about the nature of mental illness, but we have a long, long way to go.

CHRISTMAS MASSACRE

Teresa was out the morning of one Christmas Eve, making last-minute purchases for our holiday dinner.

Meanwhile, I was splayed out on the couch, in the throes of excruciating sciatica pain. That's the body's longest nerve, traveling from the lower spine to your feet. Mine was being pressured by ruptured discs. There's no physical pain quite like it. I had developed serious back problems from running and various accidents.

Next to me on the floor, I had a small safe holding all my dangerous meds. It included muscle relaxers and oxycodone, a painkiller. I kept them in a safe because I had a teenage son at home. I wasn't taking any chances with him or his friends.

I took as many Oxys, anti-inflammatories and muscle relaxers as the doctor allowed to control the pain. But it wasn't working. I couldn't get a cap on the pain, and laying down doesn't alleviate sciatic pain.

A running friend called. I didn't show up for our morning get-together. I explained the situation and she insisted on coming over.

After a few minutes there, she drove me to the emergency room at Pocono Medical Center—now called Lehigh Valley Health Network—Pocono, for treatment.

Despite the intensity of my pain, I was taken in a wheelchair to an administrative window. The clerk told me my deductible was $150 but would cut it to $135 if I paid on the spot. Here I am, in searing pain, and they are trying to make deals. Not a good sign.

After a wait, I was taken to an examination room and introduced to woman claiming to be a doctor. She had a nurse give me three shots—one, a narcotic with a name I can't remember, a non-narcotic pain med called Toradol and Valium as a muscle relaxer. I never had Valium before.

The pain wasn't going away. After a short time, I became verbally aggressive. I began cursing and yelling at the nurses and doctor when she showed up.

"The fuckin' medicine isn't working. I'm in fuckin' pain. Get the fuckin' doctor in here," I said.

Despite the haze of the drugs, my own behavior surprised me. The nurses came in several times.

"There are kids next door," they said. "If you don't stop yelling, you'll be asked to leave."

But I was out of control. Obscenities continued to spew from my mouth. Two security guards—enormous guys—came into the room.

I said, "Sure, they sent the biggest motherfuckers they could find." It's a term I had never used before. The police were called, and I was asked to leave.

Being a reporter had its benefits. I had a direct line to the hospital's CEO, and I interrupted her in a meeting to come down to help me. By the time she arrived, the two guards had escorted me out to the lobby.

The CEO met me there and got a doctor who would treat me. When I told her about what had happened, she said: "We treat people. We don't throw them out."

But she also told me I scared the people in the emergency room with my behavior. By that time the drugs were beginning to calm me down, and I was back in control.

A doctor later gave me spinal injections to alleviate the pain. At least I could walk when I left.

About two weeks later, I received a call from a police lieutenant I had become friendly with. He told me I was going to be charged with misdemeanor *fighting.*

It was a serious charge for someone who led a pretty straight life. I would need a lawyer, he told me.

I got the news during the workday. For some unknown reason it threw me into a depressive crater. All I could think about was suicide.

There was an overpass for Interstate 80 within walking distance from the office. I thought about jumping off into oncoming traffic. I remember thinking about how I would get around the protective fencing. I walked over there to assess the situation.

Watching the traffic below, I thought about the drivers, and how it might affect someone who ran me over. Or the accidents and injuries it might cause if I jumped onto the roadway.

I abandoned the idea, although the extreme depression didn't abandon me. My psychiatrist would later say the events caused post-traumatic stress disorder.

Facing charges, I sat in a small courtroom at my arraignment as other cases were called. I noticed one of the security guards from the hospital along with the female doctor sitting in a row in front of me in the courtroom. They were there to provide testimony to help the judge decide whether to hold the case over for county court. The supposed doctor was giddy. She couldn't wait to diss on me.

I was arraigned in front of a smiling judge I knew from reporting on his courtroom. It was all quite friendly. He told me I would be granted $1,000 non-cash bail, which meant I didn't have to come up with the money unless I didn't appear at the next hearing. I was in shock. Bail? I never even considered it. This was more serious than I thought.

My lawyer advised me to waive the charges and move directly to county court. That meant the two hospital employees wouldn't testify against me that day. I saw the anger on the *doctor's* face when she found out. It was worth the bail bombshell.

I eventually got my medical records from my Christmas Eve hospital visit and took them to a doctor I knew. He said the drugs they gave me could have elicited aggressive behavior. In fact, one of them had a black box warning for a possible harmful interaction with another drug I was already taking. Yet the *doctor* gave it to me anyway.

On my lawyer's advice, my doctor wrote a detailed letter to the district attorney, with exhibits detailing the possible side effects of the drugs the *doctor* gave me. He highlighted aggression and the black box interaction warning that the *doctor* ignored. The DA dropped the charges.

The hospital did a follow-up investigation by an outside doctor to understand why I was expelled instead of treated. As it turns out, the hospital had rooms where they could treat unruly patients. They never used them nor did the supposed doctor ever realize the cocktail of drugs they gave me could be creating the aggressive behavior. She probably thought I was a junkie looking for pain meds. And it turned out the woman representing herself as a doctor was a physician's assistant.

At no time during my visit did a real doctor come into the treatment room to check my status. This was confirmed by an associate who was with me in the room.

I understood from a subsequent conversation with the CEO that the report came down pretty hard on the emergency room. In a short time, the hospital changed the procedures for handling emergency patients. I'm almost certain the physician's assistant was terminated for misrepresenting herself as a doctor, in front of me, nurses and the colleague who was with me.

But the experience left me with that same feeling of helplessness, in that I was subjected to an injustice. I came to the hospital for help, lost control due to a hospital-induced drug interaction, was kicked out, and then criminally charged. A lack of control in a situation and unfair treatment are among my depression triggers. It released a greater level of sadness within me, one of helplessness, which lasted for a long time.

DEATH

My parents died a year apart when I was in my late 30s. My father died first, of a heart attack at 81. My mother died at 72 as the result of a brain stem stroke. It left her immobilized and she withered away for two weeks before succumbing to her body's fragility.

My father's death was not a surprise. He suffered from coronary artery disease and had heart bypass surgery a few years before. We expected it, and when it came, we accepted it.

But my mother's death was a shock. She had her stroke on Mother's Day. My brother tried calling her and went to her apartment to find her unconscious. She was in relatively good health and just drew a short straw.

Interestingly, neither death threw me into a deep depression. I had already learned how to deal with the constant grief of depression and had some tools to handle these developments.

Treatment can have some surprising side effects. Maybe the antidepressants I took helped to anesthetize me against the added grief. But later my reactions to other losses would argue against my belief that I was insulated from the grief of death.

A PAINFUL LOSS

Teresa and I raised our son Austin in semi-rural Pennsylvania. It is old farmland, with big houses surrounded by roosters and horse farms. The best of both worlds.

We had a yellow lab named Daisy. Typical of labs, she was as gentle as an animal could be. Devoted, obedient and completely loving. Her aim in life was to please us, and please us she did. Raised in a loving family, she had never known violence and never displayed any hostile behavior. Pure sweetness.

We had a swimming pool behind the house and Daisy loved to swim. She'd just get up from hanging out with us and take a lap in the pool. Labs are water dogs and swimming was natural for Daisy.

But she was getting up in years. Daisy was 16 and would have occasional seizures.

One summer day I was mowing the front yard with my headphones on. I noticed my next-door neighbor out of the corner of my eye, a big, muscular Russian man of about 40 running toward me. His eyes were wide, and his mouth was open.

I took off my headphones.

"There's something wrong with your dog," he said. "In the backyard."

At that moment, I noticed his family of five or so standing on a small hill overlooking our backyard, staring into it. I turned off the mower and went running toward the backyard.

As I got closer, I could hear my Teresa and Austin wailing. Both of them. Inconsolable screams of anguish. I went to the backyard and Daisy was lying lifeless next to the pool. Her limp tongue hung out of her mouth looking impossibly long.

"She drowned," Teresa said between sobs.

We scooped her up and put her in our minivan to take her to the vet in a desperate act to do something. The vet couldn't save her. Daisy was gone.

The screaming, crying by both my wife and son, along with the loss of our beloved pet, carpeted me with inconsolable grief. That is the best way I can describe the feeling of severe depression. The constant, unyielding feeling of grief. It's the heart of darkness.

In a normal situation of loss, the grief subsides as you become accustomed to the hurt. With severe depression, that feeling of despair is unshakable. It stays with you as if the loss was fresh in your mind. It's a train you can't outrun.

MASKING THE PAIN

As a writer, I often worked at home. I was in front of my computer one day in terrible psychic pain. The depression was bad. I had to get relief. Drinking was out of the question. So were drugs. I already had enough problems.

It occurred to me that if I had another sensation that was stronger than the psychic pain, it might mask it.

I reached into my pen holder, a brown wooden square cup on my shelf. In it was a dull Exacto knife, used to cut paper. I took the knife and dragged it across my forearm, between my wrist and elbow. I did it twice.

It bled profusely. Yet I sat there, looking at the blood disappointedly, thinking that it didn't hurt enough. I could still feel the pain from the depression.

I realized what I did was called cutting. I was under the impression that people who cut did it for attention. I did it exclusively for the pain. It didn't work, and I still have a scar from it today.

Yet the pain from the depression was so great that I'd do almost anything to get rid of it. I even contemplated suicide. I'd make up these scenarios in my head on how to do it to save my family embarrassment and get them some money too. I'd rent a car and drive head-on into an overpass at a high speed. That way I wouldn't ruin our car. Crazy thinking. That's where I was at. It's not that I wanted to die. I just didn't want to feel that way anymore. I resisted those thoughts. I guess I just wasn't there yet.

Cutting, or non-suicidal self-injury, I learned, usually includes cutting, scratching, carving words or symbols, self-hitting, piercing the skin with sharp objects or burning oneself. It's thought to be a way of coping with emotional pain, as was in my case.

It sometimes brings a short-term sense of relief but is often followed by feelings of guilt and shame. The painful feelings that began the cycle usually return.

The arms, legs and front of the torso are the usual targets of self-injury. It can be triggered by emotional turmoil and become a repetitive behavior. Self-injury is a signal to seek help from a professional. The injuries can progress to more significant ones and are usually an expression of unrest that should be addressed.

Being a novice do-it-yourselfer, I was always accidentally scratching or scraping myself, so it wasn't unusual to have a cut on my arm. I told my psychiatrist about it, and she just nodded. She didn't seem too concerned. I told Teresa too, and it was another burden she silently carried about my condition.

I never self-harmed after that one episode. It just didn't help relieve my feelings of sadness.

Hijinks on the Links

Following the licensing company, I ran my own direct marketing business after Teresa and I made our second residence our primary one. The business lasted a decade, but I became restless. I had also been the primary caretaker for our son, and when he started preschool, I had more time. That's when I entered the newspaper business.

I began my career in journalism as a stringer—industry terminology for a freelancer—for a small Poconos, Pennsylvania, daily newspaper. The company quickly offered me a part-time job, and after a couple of months, a full-time position.

It was the Monday afternoon of my first day as a full-timer. The newsroom received a call from an angry reader. His neighbor, a golf course owner, was hosting a private event sponsored by a topless bar. It featured exotic dancers on the golf course, and the club brought its girls and customers to the Poconos on a chartered bus.

I was given the assignment: Find out what's going on and report back. I didn't want to go. I was uncomfortable being around strippers.

But my editor told me to grab a photographer from the photo pool and take a drive down there. None of our five photographers wanted to go. I mean, what are you going to photograph for a family paper? But one kind soul finally surrendered and tagged along.

We were driving down Cherry Valley Road, a rural route which abuts the golf course. As we got within a few hundred yards of the entrance to the course, I came across a police car and two teens in the middle of the road.

The teens had a tripod-mounted video camera and were filming one of the putting green areas visible from the road. Through the trees, you could see a woman setting up a folding beach chair and stripping down from her shorts and T-shirt to a bikini.

I instantly knew that getting a copy of that video would be key. Seeing is believing, and our photographer didn't have video equipment with him.

So, I begged the kids to come to the newspaper and let us copy the video. One of them was the son of the complaining neighbor. He agreed and I crossed my fingers he would show up.

Meanwhile, the police officer was scratching his head, trying to figure out what, if any, law was being broken.

He drove his cruiser toward the golf course entrance, where the owners stationed a stocky security guard. I tucked my car behind the police car and snuck in.

I mingled with the other golfers, who were coming in from their day of play. The dancers congregated too, and I heard one say that she hoped her name didn't get in the paper, so her son wouldn't read about it. I felt like a heel.

The owner of the golf course aggressively confronted the police officer. It was a private function on private property, the owner said.

A circle of golfers formed, with police, the owner, and one undercover reporter, while this confrontation took place. I tried signaling my photographer, on the adjacent property, to take a photo of the group. The owner was well known to the community.

I returned to the newsroom and reported the scene. My editor was jubilant. Strippers on a local golf course. This was a big story. A *talker*, as we liked to say in the business.

To my relief, the kid with the video came in, and I put him together with our head photographer. We were going to get the video.

The afternoon turned to evening. Still, my editor was so excited she called in the executive editor back from his home. She said it was a big story. I wasn't so sure.

I went to my desk to write the article. After about 15 minutes, the executive editor came by and read the sole paragraph I had written. He shook his head in humorous disbelief of the facts that lay before him. But I was still a beginner in the business, and while later in my career I would have had most of a page written, I didn't know where to go.

He gave me sage advice.

"Write what you saw, what you heard, what you know."

I finished the story while the photographer was still copying the video. My editor thought we had a hit.

The next day, the headline read "Hijinks on the links."

We were hot. Our website was getting thousands of hits, and the high volume of video downloads shut down our owner Dow Jones's website servers. I was getting calls from Fox News and MSNBC to do interviews. The national cable networks were covering our local story.

I was obviously wrong about the level of interest. Exotic dancers on a golf course was novel enough to make a fascinating story. But I was right about one thing. The video was what put us over the top. Everyone wanted a peek. And all this from my first official full-time day on the job.

The excitement around the story, the accomplishment and attention put my depression in the back seat. At least for the time being. My mind was too occupied with what a hit I was, leaving little room for dark thoughts.

With my new full-time status, my head was in a pretty good place and my depression level was low at the time. The positive experience changed my affect. It wouldn't last.

The golf course was never cited.

THE NEWSROOM

Back in the newsroom, I was asked to interview, or at least try to interview, the family of a murdered male teen. It was the day after the boy's shooting death. I found his address, got in my car and headed out.

His home was a neat looking single-family house in a nice neighborhood. I assumed the family would be too distraught to talk, and just shoo me away. As a journalist, you got used to the brush-off. It's an occupational hazard.

Instead, an elderly woman answered the door. I introduced myself and my reason for being there. I said wanted to know about the boy's life, not his death. She and his family invited me in.

The boy lived with his grandmother. Over the next hour, she served me iced tea and showed me dozens of his old photographs and certificates. The pictures told the story of a kid with a normal upbringing, featuring sports clips and lots of family photos. His parents lived in New York City. It wasn't unusual to send your city child to the Poconos, where the schools were safer.

I just took it all in. I snapped off some pictures of their photos so we could use it for our story.

The grandmother was proud, appreciative and probably relieved to talk about her grandson. She was sad but resigned to the circumstances she could never have anticipated. Age has a way of doing that.

The second I arrived at the home; I went into work mod—to learn as much about this boy as I could. And then get out of there so I could write my story. The experience didn't push me into a depressed state—at least not any more than I already was. It was a job for me.

It didn't affect me any more than the day I interviewed a woman whose 60-year-old husband became the unknowing victim of a hastily planned robbery. He was delivering a Domino's pizza at 1:30 in the morning. The man was hit by a teenager's point-blank shotgun blast to the face. Yet the victim somehow survived the shooting.

My feelings took a back seat to my questions as I asked her about his final moments before the family took him off life support a day later.

The police caught the suspects within a couple of days.

Most of these experiences didn't seep into my psyche. It was work, and when I had an assignment, I was on. No emotions, only thoughts about how to get the subject to open up, the next question the reader would have and the photos I'd need.

Journalism seems to be a funny place for a depressed person to call home, but it was usually someone else's story, not mine.

THE ONES THAT STAYED WITH ME

The scanner runs 24 hours a day in the newsroom, bringing us a perpetual feed of police and fire calls from emergency 911 operators. It's a daily symphony of bells, tones and chirping voices. "Caller reports fire at 500 Main Street," "MVA at the corner of Brown and Phillips streets," and so forth.

It's usually mundane. We focus on keywords: the coroner was called, gunshots reported, multiple injuries. Those are the ones that pique our interest.

One day we heard a call—a tractor-trailer truck had a head-on collision with a passenger bus on a highway. This one would be big. I knew police would close the highway and the scene would be inaccessible. I drove to the area, on a street parallel to the highway, in the vicinity of the crash.

The yards of neat, single-family homes backed up to the highway. I looked for a home that appeared abandoned. Those weren't hard to find in the foreclosure-rich area.

I could see the emergency vehicles through the trees that acted as a barrier between the backyards and the highway. I wormed my way through the branches, scratching up my face as I moved closer to the scene. Finally, I was standing at a fence separating a backyard from the highway.

I saw the coroner there. We had gotten to know and trust each other over the years. I called out to him, and seeing the scrapes on my face, he helped me over the four-foot fence and onto the highway.

Now the chaos was right in front of me.

The crash occurred on a high-speed highway with a wide grass-covered median. The bus was traveling north, and the tractor-trailer was moving south when it drove across the median and head-on into the bus. The cab of the truck was separated from the trailer and on its side on the shoulder of the road. The bus was at a 45-degree angle on the roadway, with its side ripped open. In it, I could see several sheets covering what I later learned were bodies. It was a tourist bus carrying a group from Italy, and four people on the bus were killed.

The police there couldn't talk to me—that information is usually distributed through official means. But I could describe what I observed. And the coroner gave me the basic facts of the crash.

I drove back to my office, photos in hand, and wrote the story. I went home, and sometime afterward, it hit me. These poor innocent people, on an ordinary day trip, lost their lives so horribly and suddenly.

That one stayed with me. It took me a while to shake the sadness of what I saw and what I imagined. It triggered some depression. Despair and hopelessness. Amid the horror I dealt with frequently, it was one of the only stories that ever affected me.

AN ANGRY MAN

The other story that got to me was a particularly brutal murder. It involved a then 20-something correctional officer, Michael Parrish, who worked at the same jail where I taught once a week.

Parrish was at home taking care of his 18-month-old invalid son. The boy had a heart transplant and needed constant medications.

The mom, Parrish's live-in girlfriend, Victoria Adams, was taking a rare night off, out with her cousin and a friend. The threesome was visiting a local casino and probably having a few drinks. Michael was left to tend to the child.

As the night grew later and Victoria hadn't returned home, Parrish became angrier. When she finally arrived, he was in a rage. Her hair, he would later say, was mussed up. She must have been fooling around or something, he said. He was on edge.

Parrish also had an arsenal of guns in his home. A former skinhead, his body was tattooed with swastikas and other racist symbols. How the swastika on his neck was overlooked by the jail warden during his job interview as a correction officer would be the subject of speculation for some time.

Back in the apartment, Parrish made several accusations toward Victoria, while waving a handgun. In a moment of extreme rage, as Parrish later described it, he shot Victoria in the body and head. He then turned his gun on the little boy, shooting him in the head. Both victims were dead. Bullet casings were found in the boy's crib.

I covered the story and got to know Victoria's mother and father. I attended the funeral, on a weekend, about a week later.

Victoria's parents agreed to give me and our photographer a few minutes alone with the open casket, and our photographer shot a beautiful silhouette of the parents standing in front of the bodies. The funeral director showed me up close how he reassembled the parts of the victims' faces with silicone caulking. He was quite proud of his work.

The bodies shared a single casket. Victoria was on her back, with her son in the crook of her left shoulder, her arm around him, his hand laying on top of hers.

I just couldn't get the sight of those two bodies out of my head, especially that little boy in a casket. I sank for several weeks, wishing I had never seen what I did. I couldn't shake the depression this time, and I wish I was seeing a therapist then to talk it out. It took several years to come to terms with the impact of that experience. But I also know the victims' family will never have that luxury.

BREAKING DOWN

I reached my emotional bottom while working as a journalist. It crept up slowly but unmistakably. I don't know the cause. Work was fine and my bosses, unaware of my condition, were supportive.

The depression, always with me by this point in my life, continually worsened. Like a faucet being opened, it crescendoed, reaching a level of unbearable and unrelenting grief. The anguish enveloped me. A suffocating curtain of sadness. Surrounded by darkness, psychic pain haunted me. There were evil voices in my head. I was talking to the devil. I needed help.

The psychiatrist I was seeing recommended an outpatient program at an area hospital. I would go in the morning, stay for the day and drive home in the afternoon. No locks on the doors, no one to keep you there. It was an intermediate step on a continuum that ends with hospitalization. I'd benefit from outpatient treatment, she said, so I agreed.

I took two weeks off from work to attend the program. I didn't tell anyone where I was going or what I was doing. There were no set time limits for treatment, but my doctor thought two weeks would do it.

Checking into the program was like being on the moon. I was taken into a sparsely appointed room and sat alone at a long table. An expressionless patient arrived with a paper bag containing his clothes. He had come from the inpatient hospitalization unit.

After filling out forms, I was taken to a nurse practitioner for further intake questioning. She was a bubbly young redhead with long painted nails, caked-on makeup and tight-fitting clothes. The nurse practitioner began asking me questions: my prior history, drug usage and such. Then she asked about sex. I told her I didn't have much interest in sex, since I was one step away from being suicidal.

She giggled. "Why not? It's fun."

I couldn't believe the callousness of that comment. Here is a patient having a mental breakdown and desperate for help, and this nurse is bragging about her sex life. I came to refer to her in my head as *Nurse Ratched*, after the bitter character in "One Flew Over the Cuckoo's Nest."

Nurse Ratched was the closest thing we had to a doctor in the program. She was our go-to person for special issues. Yet, every morning, she'd come into the group room and tell us she was having a busy day. She said to try not to bother her. She despised our needs.

One time, when I suggested maybe the meds I was getting weren't working, she stopped one cold turkey. Anyone who has ever taken psych meds knows you never go cold turkey. You taper off one and slowly taper up on another one. But I was frantic. I would do anything to get rid of the grief. I followed her instructions.

She crashed me. I suffered from withdrawal symptoms, including nausea, disorienting dizziness, and paralyzing lethargy. It wasn't until I saw my regular psychiatrist after leaving the program that I got straightened out.

The daily activities in the program included group counseling, arts and crafts and mindfulness exercises. I couldn't get out of my own head. I was feeling so sick, yet all these other patients looked so outwardly normal to me.

My wife, son and I went Christmas tree shopping on the Saturday in between my treatment weeks. I was so despondent, I began to cry in the field of uncut trees, careful not to let my young son see it. He was old enough to be alarmed if he did.

One day another patient remarked that I looked normal to her — not depressed. Meanwhile, my head was filled with dread. I realized what a silent disease depression is and how we learn to project facades.

Still, I was suffering. I had to get out of my head, away from my negative thoughts. I decided that after two weeks I'd go back to work and get busy. Maybe that would take my mind off the darkness.

I returned to work. And slowly, I came out of the deep depression. I don't know why I broke down or why I recovered but it's not something I ever want to experience again.

LOCKED UP

As a district school board member, I volunteered to serve on the local vocational school board, an institution overseen by the four surrounding school districts.

One of the programs the school operated was a series of computer classes taught at the county jail. Inmates were mostly short-timers, generally serving less than five years. The classes provided training in Microsoft Office applications.

The director of adult education for the vo-tech announced the school had lost its teacher for the inmate Microsoft program. I always wanted to try teaching and was proficient in Microsoft Office, so I offered to run the class. The other board members were thrilled.

I held sessions in a small classroom at the jail. The room was also used for General Education Development (multi-purpose GED) and art classes when the jail could afford to offer it. About 12 students attended each session, because that's all the computer workstations we had.

Most of my students were minimum-security offenders, although I did have at least one convicted child molester and one murderer in the crowd. Inmates weren't always keen on discussing their offenses.

The program consisted of six sessions each of Microsoft Word, Excel and PowerPoint. I taught only one class a week, so a student could take the courses for a total of 18 weeks. I did this while I was working at the newspaper. The classes were completely voluntary. The program director at the jail even charged the inmates' commissary accounts $10 per six-week unit to help cover the cost of the textbook and to make sure they were serious about taking the course. That may sound cheap, but they were only allowed to spend 50 bucks a week if they could fund it, so it was a serious commitment. Their commissary money was mostly used to buy snacks, toiletries and, strangely enough, soup packets, which they used for gambling.

The classes were popular. It gave the inmates something to break up the boredom of the day, where they'd otherwise be sitting around in their 60-person units watching TV. And that was when they weren't locked up in their tiny—and I mean tiny—two-person cells with stainless steel, one-piece toilet-sink units. That made me pretty popular. The inmates, who I considered students, were happy someone from the outside would come in and spend time teaching them new skills and giving them a break from the tedium.

I had to learn the jail's security protocol to earn unsupervised access to the inside of the institution. To get in, I had to walk through a heavy-duty electronically controlled gate with bars. That led me into a small, monitored area with an identical gate on the other side. After the outer gate closed, the inner gate would open, giving me access to the interior. A walk down a cold, tiled hallway led to my classroom.

I always greeted the students as they entered the room. The sessions were three hours long, with two hours devoted to teaching and an hour for individual questions or projects. The computers didn't have internet access and there were no printers—it was rudimentary —but still, they got to learn some valuable skills.

Many of the inmates who opened up to me admitted they were there because they had done something stupid. That old saying that everyone in jail is innocent wasn't my experience.

The students' engagement in the class was surprisingly good, considering how their monotonous, stimulation-starved routine could turn their brains into Jell-O.

My time there didn't initially stir up my depression. Again, these were someone else's stories. I was just glad not to be one of them. Mind you, I was still depressed. But the jail didn't make it worse. At least not yet.

I didn't have security with me during the classes. This wasn't a problem since most of these students were low-level drug or alcohol offenders. But a simple altercation before the start of one of the classes reminded me of my vulnerability.

Students were filing into the classroom. The computers were set up two to a desk, so students shared a table. One student started raising his voice and getting in the face of another. Apparently, the other student moved the first student's book over a few inches to get to his workstation. Now they were standing nose to nose, on the brink of a fight. I stepped between the two of them, said a couple of conciliatory words and the tension broke. I'm sure neither of them wanted to get into a fight, but when you're confined to a small space and told what to do every minute of the day, you get protective of the few things you own. I never reported the incident to my supervisor.

One of the students I had for the full 18 weeks reminded me of retired basketball player, Magic Johnson. He was about 6 foot 4 inches tall with a smile you couldn't help but be drawn to. I can't remember why he was incarcerated. Probably drugs, as so many of the inmates were. He was a sweet guy, and I was sure the first person who would stand up to defend me if something happened in the classroom.

A couple of years after I left the jail, *Magic* got out, robbed a popular retired teacher in his home and killed the elderly man. He drove the body to South Carolina in the man's own car and dumped it on the side of the road. *Magic* was tried and convicted of murder. My confidence in judging people was shaken.

As the years went on, the surroundings in the jail began taking their toll. The confinement—I was a prisoner too while I was there—began to stir my depression.

There wasn't much of anything good in that place. Just sorry stories and individuals who'd lost their way.

I began dreading going to the jail. I gave up the job after maybe six years. It was having too much of an effect on my mood and I certainly didn't need that. Looking back, it was an odd choice of jobs, though I enjoyed seeing the excitement of a student discovering something useful. But in the end, it hurt me.

THE BULLY

When Austin was a junior in high school, his friend's house burned down. It made the news and the family scurried to find a place to live.

The boy had been a guest at our home several times for frequent sleepovers, when teens could eat junk food and play video games until all hours of the night. Teresa and Austin, my son, agreed to offer the boy a place to stay in our home until things settled down. It made sense and I was proud of my son for being willing to do it.

At the same time, one of my colleagues at the newspaper was reporting on the fire. He was looking to interview family members, deepening what might otherwise have been a one-day story.

I mentioned to the reporter that the son of the fire victim's family was planning to stay with us. The reporter wanted to talk to him. I took the reporter's cellphone number and passed it onto my son, telling my son to pass on the offer.

A few weeks later, I was called into my editor's office. She was recently promoted, a good writer, but a young and inexperienced manager. She seemed to have a chip on her shoulder for me. She once called me her nemesis because of my early successes, and she liked to make Jew jokes. As a Jew, I didn't appreciate that. She even once scolded me for interviewing an employee of a motel who saw a kitchen fire break out. The fire drew neighboring fire departments and other media outlets. The editor berated me for interviewing someone who didn't have experience with the media. *Huh?*

This time, she accused me of staging the invitation we extended to the fire victim to get my son media coverage by promoting the offer of his home to someone in need.

"This is a firing offense," she said.

I was livid. To turn around my family's simple offer of help and accuse me of self-promotion, involving my son no less, was bizarre and over the top. I had sympathy for the tragedies the editor said she experienced in her life. Yet, whatever demons she had, she seemed to deal with them by bullying me and others.

It worked. I had panicky feelings every day I'd go into the office. It stoked my depression too. It wasn't easy to get journalism positions in a shrinking job market, where newspaper posts were the victims of changing consumer information preferences. But the accusation involving Austin and this boy was the last straw.

I wrote a complaint to human resources, located in our upstate New York division headquarters. Curiously, they called me and said I shouldn't have put it in writing, since it forced them to formally act on it. I never understood that.

Eventually, HR came to my town and interviewed me about the incident. They then interviewed the editor separately. Boy, did that put a chill in the air between the editor and me since we worked closely together. It's the nature of the reporting side of the business.

HR scheduled a second meeting a couple of weeks later with both the editor and myself. Her boss, the executive editor, was also in the meeting. He was a decent guy, but never took any action to protect me from her frequent fury.

My editor apologized to me profusely in front of her boss and the two HR executives. The editor was deeply passive-aggressive, and her apology dripped with insincerity. She went overboard trying to atone for the mistake she had made. I was unmoved by her words but graciously accepted her apology. What choice did I have?

Things became a little better between the two of us after the apology. Yet, she still treated me like pigeon poop at times. She just had to have her pound of flesh.

It had, at the time, a profound effect on my psychological health. It spun me into a much deeper depression and filled me with anxiety. I spoke to people in the newsroom about it, but I think they, knowing her tendencies, were just glad they weren't her favorite target.

I'd commiserate with one reporter who was also the object of her wrath. Yet he didn't seem to react to her treatment as profoundly as I did. I was displaying something called amplification, making an incident bigger than it was. That's a part of the nature of depression.

That editor eventually took a job with another newspaper, having alienated most of those who worked with her. I heard she left that position after a brief stay, although I don't know why. But she was a cancer in the newsroom, and a feeling of relief followed her announcement to leave our paper. She actually walked out in tears, hurt because no one had taken her out to the traditional farewell lunch. No one wanted to.

A SURPRISING CAUSE OF SADNESS

I was lucky enough as a reporter to cover Barack Obama's first presidential inauguration in January 2009. The capital was buzzing with excitement—something completely new was about to happen. People unaccustomed to being empowered were getting a voice.

I drove the five-hour distance from my office the afternoon before to a friend's home in Maryland. The next day I took a 5 a.m. train into Washington, D.C., to get into the security queue for the event.

After the inauguration, I had to attend a gathering with Bob Casey, the U.S. senator from Pennsylvania. It was cold that day. I wore a suit for the senator's get-together, layering all the clothes I had on top of it to survive the long cold wait on that security line.

Following the ceremonies, I attended the senator's get-together in the Senate Office Building. Then I took a train back to my car, changed my clothes and headed straight to a Panera Bread restaurant to write two stories about the inauguration. I finished at about 9 p.m. and emailed them with photos to my editor. Then began the five-hour drive home, resting once at a truck stop to close my eyes. A working girl came up to my window and asked me if I wanted a date.

The inauguration was on a Tuesday. After arriving home early Wednesday morning, I went to work Wednesday and Thursday. I became sick as a dog. I took Friday off. My doctor sent me to the hospital for tests. On my way home, I fell asleep, and my car ran across a country roadway, hitting a tree.

I was driving an old Jeep Wrangler without airbags or a working driver's side seat belt. My head broke the windshield on the initial impact with the tree. As the car began to tip over on the driver's side into a ditch, my head snapped back into the headrest, bounced forward and broke the windshield again. The car was totaled, and I was unconscious.

I spent three days in the hospital bruised and concussed. During my second day, the phone next to my bed rang. I reached over to answer it and a sharp burning pain stabbed me in the back. I screamed. A nurse ran in and dosed my IV with morphine.

After years of long-distance running and the spine-crushing car accident, I developed back problems. That led to chronic pain, which in turn led to more depression. My problem was herniated discs, the jellylike substance that cushions the vertebrae in your spine and acts as shock absorbers. Some of my shock-absorbing material seeped out from between the vertebrae and was useless. I also suffered from compression of my spinal cord that required surgery.

The constant pain wore on me, sinking me into greater sadness. I took painkillers but those barely diminished the discomfort. I stopped taking them after a while—these drugs were getting too much bad press.

It's been reported that between one-quarter to more than half of those who complain to their doctors of pain are depressed. A person is more likely to become depressed when pain limits activities and independence.

The pain lessened after my first spinal surgery in 2016, but I still felt it every day. And it kept me from doing things I used to love, like running or skiing. It aggravated my depression. But I wasn't aware of that connection...Yet.

What is Depression?

D epression is a serious medical illness that negatively affects how you feel, the way you think and how you act, according to the American Psychiatric Association. But it's more than feeling lousy.

Depression encompasses many symptoms and affects people differently. The most common symptoms include disinterest, lethargy, sadness, and detachment. Motivation goes down the toilet. Some people feel that life isn't worth living. Others feel emotionally flat or numb, worthless or guilty, and experience heightened anxiety.

Feelings of depression can impact your behavior in many ways, including:[1]

- Loss of pleasure in activities
- Loss of sexual interest
- Changes in appetite or weight
- Impaired thinking or concentration
- Moving or talking more slowly
- Restlessness

---

[1] Depression (major depressive disorder), Mayo Clinic, 2020

- Difficulty making decisions
- Loss of self-esteem
- Sleep problems
- Physical aches and pains

Feeling sad or grief-ridden doesn't mean you're depressed. It's natural when life's losses and disappointments bring on these feelings.

Depression is different. It's when these feelings last more than a couple of weeks. And depression usually causes social dysfunction in you, including isolation and withdrawal. Major depression is different. The diagnosis is used when low mood is accompanied by at least five of these symptoms or behaviors.

If you experience fewer, say two to four of these symptoms, you may have a less severe depression, called subsyndromal symptomatic depression.[2] Yet mild symptoms could lead to more severe depression. Doctors advise you alert them to these symptoms and remain in tune with your mental status. Depression is known to be highly treatable. But it's far from the vaccine stage.

If you are having thoughts of suicide, call the National Suicide Prevention Lifeline at 1-800-273-8255 (TALK). You can find a list of additional resources at SpeakingOfSuicide.com/resources.

---

[2] National Institute of Mental Health, Depression, https://www.nimh.nih.gov/health/topics/depression/index.shtml

RISKY BUSINESS

All my calamities—the car crash when I was too tired to drive, the many activities that led to concussions and even the hospital outburst— could have the same common denominator.

Those who are depressed are known to display risky behaviors. Drugs, alcohol, gambling and cutting are the most common. Some think of these as quick fixes for the pain. These are, of course, only temporary ways to cover up the misery. Doing these things can be rewarding at the moment. It may, for a short time, allow us to forget about our problems.

I have another point of view. When I was deeply depressed, which was most of the time, I just didn't care if I got hurt. I wasn't fearless. I was ambivalent. It allowed me to ski trails way over my head at speeds I had no business traveling. Or drive when I had too many drinks. Or putting myself in other dangerous situations.

Marathoning was probably part of that. Taking it to the edge as a big guy, pushing my body as hard as I could for decades and not caring about the consequences was risky behavior. Year after year. Two back and two knee surgeries later have put perspective on those decisions. But not at the time.

Depression has also been linked to sexually risky behaviors. I can't say it's not true for me, but who didn't have unprotected sex in the 1970s and early '80s. I do think it was part of my pattern of risk-taking, though.

RAGE

My son played youth soccer. We signed him up for a friendly local league and got to know the other parents and kids. The team stayed together for years, and it was as social as it was athletic.

My son was a second-tier player—just beyond the bubble of a starter. He seemed to take it in stride, and we sucked it up too. There were some good players on that team.

The team lost its first game badly. To pump up morale, my wife set up a tailgate for the kids after the games. In her mind, it would soften the blow for losing. We had music and food. The kids loved it, although the parents tired of their responsibilities to help supply the tailgate.

After several years, the kids were aging out of the league. The next step, if there was to be one, would be the school team. The league games were coming to a close.

Our final game was during a tournament that pitted teams from outside the area. It would be the last time the team played together.

I wanted my son to go out on a high note and called the coach to ask if she'd start him in this final game. We had become close to the coach over the years and socialized often. It was a small request, so I thought.

The coach explained to me how she got those types of calls often—parents wanting their child to be a starter. She said she couldn't do it. I was stunned. We had done a lot for this coach and the team over the years, and in my mind, it was a small and simple request. Send him off with some extra confidence since he probably wouldn't pursue soccer after this game.

I was at work and argued. In the openness of a newsroom, no conversations are private. I raised my voice and began to get personal. I just couldn't believe she wouldn't accommodate this one request—I had never asked for one before. I brought the exchange to a pitched level, refusing to take no for an answer. Anger spewed from my mouth. I could feel my blood pressure rise and my language fall into a series of profanities. I was out of control with rage.

As I was talking to the coach on my cellphone, my desk phone rang. It was my then-editor, an optimistic, enthusiastic professional.

"Can you come to the conference room," he asked sternly.

"In a minute," I said.

Then I got back to my call with the coach and continued to argue uncontrollably. My anger rose. The coach argued back, but her voice trembled with the shock that a good friend would go ballistic on her. She stood her ground, but I am sure she was thinking, *This isn't happening.*

My phone rang again. It was my editor. Again, he asked me to come to the conference room. This time his speech deepened and slowed, carrying more authority and urgency.

After a few more minutes on the phone with the coach, I got off and walked into the conference room. My editor was sitting there, looking at me with a mix of seriousness and incredulity.

I was breathless, could feel my heart beating fast, and my face felt flushed red. I was in a zone of irrationality. I had just lambasted a good friend in a full voice in front of my associates for more than a half an hour.

To his credit, my editor just wanted me to calm down. He said he couldn't allow that type of behavior in the newsroom. It wasn't a warning, just a justification for getting me out of the situation. He helped me avoid taking the conversation to deeper depths.

I came out of the trance and went on with my work. The coach came into the office the next day in tears to talk, yet I was over it and in a normal mood. I apologized for my outburst, and it seemed to calm her down. In retrospect, I was like Hannibal Lecter one day and Forrest Gump the next.

Surprisingly, the coach started my son in the game. It was probably his best performance of his youth soccer career. Yet it came at an inexcusable cost.

This was the worst anger outburst I could ever remember but not the only one. Anger is often a byproduct of depression and I obviously had it bad. I expressed it mostly at home, to my wife and son. It created a *walking on eggshells* type of atmosphere at times. Those were not my best moments. My wife even now hesitates to bring up those times.

We are still close with that coach after all these years. And I still carry the guilt for my reckless behavior.

PAPA BEAR

A familiar soccer mom stopped by the newsroom early one summer morning. Our children, about 8 years old, were in a summer camp together. The mom came to tell me that the day before, Austin had told her son he was going to kill him. When she dropped her own son off at camp that morning, she said she admonished Austin for what he apparently said. I was OK with that, thinking it was a reasonable reaction to my son's behavior. Yet, she appeared drunk.

She'd been known to show up acting unusual at soccer games. Our kids played on the same team. Still, I didn't think much about it. If my son said something dumb, I trusted another parent to say something to him about it.

A few minutes later, I got a call from the camp to come down. They told me an incident had occurred and I needed to be there.

When I arrived, the police were there. They told me this mom opened up on Austin and screamed at him loud enough for all the counselors to hear. It scared my son so badly he wet himself. The officer cited the mother for disorderly conduct.

The camp gave my son a change of clothes but because of the nature of the incident and police presence, the camp thought I needed to know.

The police officer warned the mother to stay away from my son. I took that seriously. Since the boys were on the same soccer team, they'd be in close proximity. I wanted her to be banned from the games. I lobbied the soccer coach unsuccessfully to ban the mother from the games. The coach agreed to talk to the mother and tell her to keep her distance from my son. I didn't want him intimidated.

I couldn't let go of my anger. It consumed me. I wanted this mother far away from my son, which is not easy to do on a soccer sideline. Teresa wasn't as upset. It was an incident to her, and the bigger deal I made of it, the worse it would be for Austin, she later told me.

That anger has been a trademark of my depression. It consumed me in the incident with my brother, the soccer coach and the bully boss. Walking around with so much rage clearly lowered the quality of my life. Now that my depression is under better control, the anger isn't as dominant in my thoughts. But it's still there.

PARANOIA

Austin, now a teenager, was standing with my wife at the sink in the kitchen, preparing a dinner. He adopted her love of cooking, and they often made meals together. When I saw that, I got angry. I was excluded from the conversation and work. They didn't want me helping, and I was sure they were talking about me.

They weren't, of course, and my lack of participation was a reflection of my apathy toward all things besides eating. My wife would later say, "You always thought we were plotting against you."

Paranoia is a common symptom of depression. It's part of the mechanism of distorting reality, which is a keystone of the disease. That includes seeing, hearing, or believing things that aren't real.

Mental Health America defines paranoia as intense anxious or fearful feelings and thoughts often related to persecution, threat or conspiracy. I always leaned toward Richard Nixon's definition as *heightened awareness.*

The bully editor at the newspaper filled me with paranoia about my job security. I was wrapped in an anxious knot all day worrying about her motivations. I examined each of her words and actions through this distortion. I felt she was trying to get rid of me, even though she never did.

Paranoia can be crippling, as it was for me for a time at the newspaper. I took more anxiety pills; Clonazepam I believe it was. I dreaded the work that I loved.

My paranoia is still there, my mind distorting my perceptions of the real world. But being aware of this allows me to do reality checks and keep the paranoia from influencing my behaviors. And by controlling my thoughts, it helps me control my emotions. It's the basis of cognitive behavioral therapy.

THE ULTIMATE THREAT

I carried a lot of anger and paranoia with my depression. I guess I was angry about being depressed, and my family took the brunt of the fury. But there was more to the anger. I don't know where it came from, and years of counseling never answered that question.

I walked down from my bedroom one evening to the living room where my wife was watching TV. I was in a particularly depressed mood—hopeless and in pain—and for some reason I told her I took a bunch of meds to overdose. At the time she knew I had ample supplies of drugs, including painkillers for my back like Oxycodone, and sedatives like Clonazepam, a benzodiazepine for anxiety.

Teresa took off out the front door, shoeless and in her pajamas. She began sprinting down our long driveway, trying to figure out what to do. During her dash, she later told me, she decided to go to a neighbor's house, a retired doctor, and ask for help.

I got into our Jeep and went chasing after her, riding on the lawn alongside the driveway. I tried to stop her. I assured her I didn't take anything. Eventually, she got into the Jeep and returned to the house with me.

It was one of many times I threatened suicide. It was always in the air. Teresa would tell me how hurtful those words were to her, but I never internalized that emotion. I didn't understand the effect on her. I was just screaming for help, for relief from the pain.

Years later, she told me she had spent the past couple of decades keeping me from killing myself.

The problem was, I warned her if she ever called the police about my threats, they'd lock me up in a mental ward, and it would become a part of my permanent public record. An involuntary commitment. That, in turn, could hurt any future job searches. It was a Catch-22 for her.

She never did call the police. God knows, she had every right to. I just wanted to stop the pain and I didn't know how.

My depression had profound effects on our relationship. She told me years later if it had not been for our son that she would have left me a long time ago. I can see it. All she wanted to do was get our son through high school.

My depression came with a fair amount of paranoia. Jealous of the close relationship my wife had with our son, I was always accusing them of plotting against me. In my mind, it was two against one. A private club in which I didn't have membership.

Those feelings of anger and paranoia eased some once my medications were better balanced. But I can't honestly say I'm beyond feelings of paranoia, at home and in the workplace. And my anger sometimes got the better of me at home, where it's safe.

RELATIONSHIPS

Teresa and I discussed my depression over lunch recently. I wanted her to recall incidents where she thought my depression had reared its ugly head. She became increasingly angry as she talked about episodes of my anger and inappropriate behavior. It wasn't a pleasant conversation. But I asked, so I sat there and took it all without reacting.

My depression has mortally wounded our relationship. My anger and irritability created tension. She has so much disdain for my behavior and stopped caring why I behaved the way I did.

It just wasn't the deal she thought she was getting into when we agreed to live together and get married. I wasn't the package that was promised. And it's true. Although I believe I had severe depression all along, my symptoms got worse over time. And even though it's responded somewhat to my current mix of medications, she can't let go of the past. Or the present.

I've become a recluse, happy to be alone. I don't initiate conversation socially, nor respond well to her small talk. And I don't go out. I'm unlikely to do things that most people enjoy—like bike rides or going out to a movie. I've become a dud.

I go to the gym three or four times a week—but that's really to appease my wife and son, who wanted me to stay physically healthy. I get no enjoyment out of it. That is a change for me. I was addicted to running and loved being in shape.

My wife didn't love the addiction—it took a lot of time and eventually, a toll on my body. But it was better than being inactive and overweight, where I now find myself.

Depression had another effect on me. It made me ultra-sensitive to the comments and actions of others, including those of my wife. Teresa is a tough-skinned woman, and often makes distressing comments or criticisms about my appearance or behavior that trigger my ultrasensitive nature. I guess she thinks I'd be able to slough them off like she does.

I remember one of my psychology professors describing a somewhat rare personality type as perfectly adjusted. I think Teresa fits that category.

I don't. I react with hurt, followed by anger and verbal reprisals. It has made our relationship toxic. We still work toward the same goals, but interpersonally, there's friction.

That element of anger is a common denominator for me in relationships. In my high school/college relationship, I was abusive out of anger. Now I'm verbally abusive. It's hurt my relationship intensely.

I've been with Teresa for almost 40 years now, although we took a short break after about a year or two. I saw other women during that time and I'm sure my mood didn't impress anyone. No one stuck, and that was before my symptoms got worse.

I think I carried an overtone of bleakness. Not an appealing quality.

ATTRACTION

I dated several women when Teresa and I took a couple of years apart. Friends were more than willing to hook me up with their own single friends. They thought I was a catch, I guess. A young professional, physically fit and decent looking.

I never discussed my depression with anyone. In fact, it wasn't until that ultimatum my girlfriend gave me years later that the word depression entered my vocabulary. So, naturally, it didn't come up on these dates, which never lasted more than a few outings. The subject wouldn't have come up. I just wasn't that self-aware.

And later, after I came to terms with my illness, I became acutely aware of the stigma mental health issues carried. If I were to have dated later in my life, I would have had to be pretty close to someone to risk exposing my dark side. But of course, by then, they themselves would have sensed something was wrong. My insecurity, moodiness and struggles with everyday events would have tipped them off.

Maybe because of my depression, I wasn't attracted to someone with their own insecurities. I had enough of my own and couldn't support someone else's issues, so strong women appealed to me. That turned out to be my eventual wife.

THE CUCKOO'S NEST

Meanwhile, working as a journalist, my depression was getting worse. My doctor tried new combinations of medicines. Most of us know changing psych meds is slow and painful. You have to ramp up on the new one and taper off the old one. It takes weeks for it to take effect. If it does at all. Yet you need and want relief right away.

I had been through all the usual suspects: Prozac. Effexor. Zoloft. Paxil. Wellbutrin. Lexapro. I lost count. None worked well enough. Mine was described as a treatment-resistant depression.

Now I was ready for the big time, Lithium. Another step down the rabbit hole of mental illness treatment and an escalation of my status as a mentally ill person.

Lithium is used for bipolar disorder, depression and schizophrenia. It's the big leagues of psychopharmaceutical drugs. The problem was, Lithium must be closely monitored through blood tests. I would have to increase my dosage a little, take a blood test, have the doctor evaluate it, and then decide to begin the cycle all over again. It would take a long time—weeks—to get up to a therapeutic dosage. The thought of the wait was intolerable.

My psychiatrist had a solution. Why not enter an inpatient program in a hospital where they could test my blood every day? That way they could adjust the Lithium levels until they reached therapeutic levels. Wow, inpatient psychiatric care—talk about a big step up the treatment hierarchy.

But again, I was desperate, so I agreed. I promised my doctor I'd check in. I'm not sure she believed I'd go. I packed a bag and headed to the hospital that evening. She said to tell the emergency room front desk clerk that I was there for a behavioral evaluation. That would trigger a rapid and well-rehearsed procedure. They'd take me back to a room immediately without waiting. As promised, I said the words and was whisked back to a treatment area.

I waited quite a while in an examination room with just a gurney and chair. A nurse came in and asked me some questions. She balked when I didn't say I was contemplating suicide. The hospital wouldn't have admitted me if I didn't say I was. So, I did. Just to get that Lithium.

Eventually I was taken upstairs to what I suppose was the psych floor. It must have been. The doors to the floor were locked from the inside. I met with the hospital psychiatrist, and we laid out a plan. In the meantime, I spent my days waiting on line for meds—a routine repeated several times a day—seeing the psychiatrist and in various therapy sessions.

Then there were arts and crafts. Everyone's favorite period. I guess that's because it focuses you on mindfulness, taking your thoughts off the negative thinking that clouds your consciousness.

I painted a birdhouse and made a pink piggy bank. I noticed that a group of other patients joined me at my table one day. It was probably because I wasn't suffering as much as they were. They were attracted to my upbeat attitude toward painting that piggy bank.

My stay only lasted three days. They couldn't keep me any longer because I wasn't suicidal. I never did get the Lithium up to therapeutic levels. My blood diluted it too much. It was back to the drawing board.

SHOCK TO THE SYSTEM

I was still seeking relief from this horrible depression that I just couldn't shake. The doctor had put me through a bunch more meds that didn't provide relief. It was time for the next step.

She recommended electroconvulsive therapy (ECT). That's where they put a wand to your head and send voltage through your brain while you're under anesthesia. It's supposed to induce a convulsion and reboot your brain. It was, yet again, another step up the treatment ladder and another downgrading of my self-image. ECT is supposed to be quite effective. But it was the worst experience of my treatment.

I had to be at the hospital at 5 a.m. for prep. They do typical testing like blood pressure and heart rate. You change into a hospital gown. They hook you up to an IV. Then you wait.

Eventually, someone comes and wheels you into this cavernous treatment space, with a dozen adjacent medical stations. A grumpy male nurse with coiffed hair would tug open my hospital gown, treating me like a rag doll. He'd stick a bunch of electrodes on my chest and foot. I'm sure the other patients alongside me were handled in the same rough manner.

At this point, eight or 10 patients were lined up in the treatment area, one adjacent to the next, on gurneys, with just a partial curtain separating each one. There was no privacy. It was an assembly line for ECT. Then the doctor would come in with his team, which included technicians and an anesthesiologist. One by one, he'd go down the line and repeat the process. Ask you how you were and have the anesthesiologist put you under.

One of the technicians would call out "voltage."

The doctor would call "Clear!" and an alternating two-note bell sound would play while the voltage was applied. They'd do several in a row while you waited your turn. It was medieval.

I'd wake up in a private treatment cubicle, feeling wiped out. My wife was there and would take me home. I spent the rest of the day spaced out and without any relief from the depression.

I had a bad reaction to one of the treatments. I woke up with a feeling of dread and complete darkness. When they got the doctor, I told him I wasn't safe.

Safe was a code word we used in the out-treatment center. It was a way of letting everyone know at the end of the day we'd be OK for the night. I knew after this treatment something was exceedingly wrong.

The doctor admitted me to the hospital's psych ward for the weekend. My wife visited. She remembered people walking around aimlessly. I wasn't much better.

"You were out of it," she later said. The doctor never gave me an explanation for my reaction.

I had about 15 ECT treatments. When I told the doctor I still felt depressed, he said I needed more treatments. No consideration was ever given toward whether or not the therapy was working for me.

ECT failed to reduce my depressive symptoms and it wiped out my short-term memory. That's supposed to last only as long as the treatment lasts. But I also think it has affected my memory in the longer term. I just can't seem to recall events that occurred only months before.

My wife, on the other hand, thinks I improved as a result of the treatments. While I understand many people benefit from the treatment, I regret it.

BRAIN GAMES

I embrace the darkness. No, not in a psychological way. I mean dark rooms. Rainy days. Bright sunlight irritates my eyes. There may be a reason for this. God knows, my depression could explain it. But there's another possibility, which led me to a new treatment.

My son was 4 years old, and my wife wanted to take him to an ice-skating rink. Saddled with depression, I didn't want to go. But she convinced me, promising to take him on the ice herself.

When we got there, things changed. She no longer wanted to skate and asked me to. Neither of us knew how to skate but I agreed and flopped around the ice.

An employee eventually gave me a barrel to hold onto, making it easier to skate. My son had no problem. He picked it right up and glided around the oval rink somewhat awkwardly.

At one point I must have lost my balance. As my wife described it, I jerked backwards and flailed my arms. Overcompensating for my lack of stability, I lurched forward and smashed my forehead into the ice. My feet went limp, and it was obvious I was out.

The first thing I remember was hearing the cries of my son. A pool of blood spilled out around my head as I laid motionless on the ice. I heard the voice of a nurse, telling me I was going to be OK.

I kept asking if that was my son crying and what had happened. My repetitive questions were a sign of a possible brain bleed. They called in a medevac helicopter to take me to the nearest level-one trauma center about 40 miles away.

An ambulance took me to a clearing, where the helicopter was waiting. By then I was more lucid and kept asking questions of the two EMS technicians on the helicopter. I could tell by the serious look on one their faces that my injury might be worse than I thought.

We arrived at the hospital and a team of doctors checked me out in the emergency room. I couldn't feel my feet and was worried that the fall might have affected my lower extremities.

The doctor rubbed my toes and told me it was just numb from the cold. The ice-skating arena took my rental skates off of my feet before I was taken away and the temperature in the helicopter cabin must have been chilly.

The tests showed I didn't have a brain bleed and would be OK. A few stitches and a shot of painkiller later, I was up in a room to spend the night under observation. The New York Giants football team was playing the San Francisco 49ers in the playoffs in 2002 and I had nothing but time, a headache and a deli sandwich to watch the game. It did hurt to chew.

It was one of several concussions I had, many of them within a 15-year period. I got hit by a baseball bat once, lost consciousness while slamming my head skiing and slipped in an icy parking lot, hitting the back of my head, another knockout. I was in that car accident, with a loss of consciousness when my head broke the windshield twice, another hospitalization, and was hit by a biker while running in Central Park. That time the impact drove me to the ground, and with my luck, headfirst. Again, I lost consciousness and was hospitalized.

Later, I started experiencing headaches and extreme light and sound sensitivity. For a while I had to write in a darkened, unused office near the newsroom. I also experienced forgetfulness and occasional disorientation. And, of course, I had depression. Something wasn't right.

My wife took me to a neurologist at New York University's Langone Medical Center on the east side of Manhattan. She had read of a specialist there who helped a woman with some of the same symptoms.

The neurologist put me through a number of cognitive and radiative tests. One test, called single-photon emission computed tomography (SPECT) mapped the blood flow in my brain.

He showed us the film. There were white spots on the image, indicating areas my brain wasn't getting blood. He said it could suggest inflammation or a viral infection.

I spent the next week in the hospital's epilepsy center. The idea was to infuse me with massive amounts of anti-inflammatories and antivirals. I'd have four 90-minute infusions a day, evenly spaced out during the 24-hour period. The anti-inflammatory, a cousin of prednisone, would spike my blood sugar, so I had to get an injection of insulin before each treatment.

In the meantime, a technician pasted about a dozen electrodes to my head, which were held down by a heavy wool knit hat. It was summertime and that hat was hot. I had to wear it 24 hours a day so technicians could monitor my brain waves.

The tether of electrodes was just long enough to let you reach the bathroom and door to your room. I remember peeking out of the doorway one day and seeing another patient with this ridiculous gnarl of wires spilling out from under his hat.

I continued the infusion treatment on an outpatient basis after leaving the hospital. It didn't make me sick, but I always got an unpleasant metallic taste in my mouth during the procedure.

The treatment helped. My light and auditory sensitivity retreated. My disorientation and forgetfulness improved. And for a time, my depression improved. A doctor friend of ours said it was common to feel some euphoria after taking corticosteroids. Unfortunately, it didn't last.

I've suffered additional concussions since. None requiring hospitalization but at one time a psychiatrist thought I might have the beginnings of chronic traumatic encephalopathy (CTE). That's the degenerative brain disease usually suffered by boxers and football players who have experienced multiple head traumas. There's not much I can do about that. I continued focusing on the depression and getting better.

RUNING AWAY FROM DEPRESSION

I first met Teresa at that jeans company when I was 24. I thought she was a knockout and I wanted to take her out.

She told me she ran in Central Park. Running was not my thing. I never even tried it. But if this girl ran, then I was going to run. It would be a good excuse to spend some time together. Or just impress her.

I spent the next week trying to learn how to run. I used a track at a nearby community college, doing quarter-mile laps and sucking wind in my flat-bottom, white basketball shoes.

I was already fit. After a week, I was able to run a few miles, although not easily. I asked my colleague if she wanted to run one day after work, and she agreed.

We did a four-mile loop in Central Park in New York City. I flopped around one step at a time in those basketball shoes. I remember seeing the stoplight in the park where our finish would be and silently prayed that it would come sooner rather than later.

In the process, I became hooked. Running developed into a staple for our relationship. We ran almost every day after work. I bought real running shoes, and it was actually enjoyable. A time for good conversation and developing our friendship while touring the various ethnicities that symbolize the different parts of the park.

My running eventually graduated to races, and ultimately, marathons. I got the fever and ended up doing 12 New York City Marathons by the time I hit my mid-40s. My wife even did one with me.

Running was a distraction for my depression. It puts you in the moment. It's hard to feel depressed when you're struggling to put one foot in front of the other, ignore the leg pain and shortness of breath. Running also releases endorphins, your body's counterpart to morphine. It gives you a sensation of well-being and a general feeling of euphoria.

The feeling doesn't last forever, of course, but the knowledge that you put in a good run does. You feel fitter physically and healthier mentally.

Unfortunately, life's turns have made running impossible for me now. I've tried walking but that doesn't give me the same satisfaction. Or high. I've threatened to use an elliptical machine that doesn't create an impact on my back. I tried it once and learned how out of shape I am. Maybe I'll give it another try. But there's no doubt that regular, intensive exercise eased my depression.

SPECIAL K

In the winter of 2019, I became aware of a new treatment for depression that had just been approved by the U.S. Food and Drug Administration. It is called ketamine, an older drug used as an anesthetic.

Ketamine is related to a club party drug, called Special K, when used in larger dosages. Special K is part of a class of club drugs known for lowering inhibition, impairing judgment and increasing sexual risk-taking. It was thought to target a part of the brain no current antidepressants did.

Ketamine is the first new antidepressant medication with a novel mechanism of action since the 1980s, Janine Simmons, M.D., Ph.D., and chief of the National Institute of Mental Health Social and Affective Neuroscience Program, said. Its ability to rapidly decrease suicidal thoughts was believed to be a fundamental breakthrough. Additional insights into ketamine's longer-term effects on brain circuits could guide future advances in the management of mood disorders.

I was excited about the news. It was meant for those who are treatment resistant — just like me. Though the success rate was low — about 20 percent -- it was still a chance, and I had to go for it.

Fortunately, the psychiatry practice I was going to planned to implement the treatment. Just not right away.

The drug is a high-maintenance therapy. You have to have it administered by a doctor every few weeks and stay for a couple of hours to be observed for dissociative behavior. What the hell. It was worth a try. I waited for the treatment to become available. And I waited.

More than a year later, I was told about procedural difficulties in administering the drug at the health network. They still hadn't worked out the exact methodology, like who would be in charge of it and how it would happen workflow-wise. You'd think they could figure that out. Unfortunately, it never came, so I'm still waiting.

Cognitive Behavioral Therapy

I've tried several types of talk therapy at the urging of my psychiatrists. Cognitive Behavioral Therapy (CBT) is one of the most common and widespread today and one I've been through. It addresses inaccurate or negative thinking, which in turn affects your emotions and, eventually, behaviors.

According to the Mayo Clinic, CBT is often the chosen approach to psychotherapy because it can quickly help identify and cope with specific challenges. And CBT often requires fewer sessions than other types of therapy.

The Mayo Clinic says it may help to:

- Manage symptoms of mental illness
- Prevent a relapse of mental illness symptoms
- Treat a mental illness when medications aren't a good option
- Learn techniques for coping with stressful life situations
- Identify ways to manage emotions

- Resolve relationship conflicts and learn better ways to communicate
- Cope with grief or loss
- Overcome emotional trauma related to abuse or violence
- Cope with a medical illness
- Manage chronic physical symptoms

Here's how CBT works: It changes people's attitudes and behaviors by looking at and challenging the veracity of underlying thoughts and beliefs. And then it examines how these relate to a person's behavior, as a way of dealing with emotional problems. The goal is to change patterns of thinking or behavior behind someone's problems, and therefore change the way they feel.

I have gone through CBT therapy for a few years. It's a hard lesson for me to learn, since the demons are always talking to me. It's a struggle for me and my particular brand of depression, yet I understand and acknowledge the logic and potential for the therapy. And it's helped in many situations. If I have an unpleasant reaction to a situation, I try to break down the reality or fact sets and question them. But maybe I needed to go back for a refresher course.

COGNITIVE DISTORTIONS

Unhealthy thinking sometimes involves ways our minds convince us of something that isn't really true. That's cognitive distortion. Inaccurate thoughts usually reinforce negative thinking or emotions. We tell ourselves things that seem accurate and rational but really only keep us feeling bad about ourselves.

Many cognitive-behavioral and other kinds of therapists try to help a person learn to change cognitive distortions in psychotherapy. It's an essential element in CBT.

Dr. David Burns defined 10 patterns of cognitive distortions in a handout for the Pennsylvania Child Welfare Resource Center in 2000. I found these to be quite helpful:

1. <u>All-or-Nothing Thinking</u>: You see things in black-or-white categories. If a situation falls short of perfect, you see it as a total failure. When a young woman on a diet ate a spoonful of ice cream, she told herself," I've blown my diet completely." This thought upset her so much that she gobbled down an entire quart of ice cream!

2. <u>Over-generalization</u>: You see a single negative event, such as a romantic rejection or a career reversal, as a never-ending pattern of defeat by using words such as *always* or *never* when you think about it. A depressed salesman became terribly upset when he noticed bird dung on the windshield of his car. He told himself," Just my luck! Birds are always crapping on my car!"

3. <u>Mental Filter</u>: You pick out a single negative detail and dwell on it exclusively, so that your vision of all reality becomes darkened, like the drop of ink that discolors a beaker of water. Example: You receive many

positive comments about your presentation to a group of associates at work but one of them says something mildly critical. You obsess about his reaction for days and ignore all the positive feedback.

4. <u>Discounting the Positive</u>: You reject positive experiences by insisting they *don't count*. If you do a good job, you may tell yourself that it wasn't good enough or that anyone could have done as well. Discounting the positive takes the joy out of life and makes you feel inadequate and unrewarded.

5. <u>Jumping to Conclusions</u>: You interpret things negatively when there are no facts to support your conclusion.

> Mind Reading: Without checking it out, you arbitrarily conclude that someone is reacting negatively to you.

> Fortune-telling: You predict that things will turn out badly. Before a test you may tell yourself, "I'm really going to blow it. What if I flunk?" If you're depressed you may tell yourself, "I'll never get better."

6. <u>Magnification</u>: You exaggerate the importance of your problems and shortcomings, or you minimize the importance of your desirable qualities. This is also called the "binocular trick."

7. <u>Emotional Reasoning</u>: You assume that your negative emotions necessarily reflect the way things really are: "I feel terrified about going on airplanes. It must be very dangerous to fly." Or "I feel guilty. I must

be a rotten person." Or "I feel angry. This proves I'm being treated unfairly." Or "I feel so inferior. This means I'm a second-rate person." Or "I feel hopeless. I must really be hopeless."

8. "Should" statements: You tell yourself that things should be the way you hoped or expected them to be. After playing a difficult piece on the piano, a gifted pianist told herself, "I shouldn't have made so many mistakes." This made her feel so disgusted that she quit practicing for several days. *Musts, oughts,* and *have tos* are similar offenders.

Should statements that are directed against yourself lead to guilt and frustration. Should statements that are directed against other people or the world in general lead to anger and frustration: "He shouldn't be so stubborn and argumentative."

Many people try to motivate themselves with should and shouldn'ts, as if they were delinquents who had to be punished before they could be expected to do anything. "I shouldn't eat that doughnut." This usually doesn't work because all these *should* and *musts* make you feel rebellious and you get the urge to do just the opposite. Dr. Albert Ellis has called this *musterbation.* I call it the *shouldy* approach to life.

9. Labeling: Labeling is an extreme form of all-or-nothing thinking. Instead of saying "I made a mistake," you attach a negative label to yourself: "I'm a loser." You might also label yourself "a fool" or "a failure" or "a jerk." Labeling is quite irrational because you are not the same as

what you do. Human beings exist, but "fools," "losers" and "jerks" do not. These labels are just useless abstractions that lead to anger, anxiety, frustration and low self-esteem.

10. <u>Personalization and blame</u>: Personalization occurs when you hold yourself personally responsible for an event that isn't entirely under your control. When a woman received a note that her child was having difficulties at school, she told herself, "This shows what a bad mother I am," instead of trying to pinpoint the cause of the problem so that she could be helpful to her child. When another woman's husband beat her, she told herself, "If only I were better in bed, he wouldn't beat me." Personalization leads to guilt, shame and feelings of inadequacy.

Some people do the opposite. They blame other people or their circumstances for their problems, and they overlook ways that they might be contributing to the problem: "The reason my marriage is so lousy is because my spouse is totally unreasonable." Blame usually doesn't work very well because other people will resent being scapegoated and they will just toss the blame right back in your lap. It's like the game of hot potato — no one wants to get stuck with it.

The Resilience Alliance, which focuses on behavioral health, suggests reframing strategies to deal with cognitive distortion: Explore what's stressing you: View your situation with positive eyes. Find what you can change: If you could, what parts of your situation would you most like to change? With positive reframing, you may see possibilities you weren't aware of before.

Identify benefits: Find the benefits in the situation you face. Discover the humor: Find the aspects of your situation that are so absurd that you can't help but laugh.

I am guilty of several of these cognitive distortions and have worked at recognizing the times I'm using them so I can alter my thinking and emotions. I find it's a constant battle. But it does help. I highly recommend learning about these.

POSITIVE THERAPY

More recently, I began seeing a therapist who practices a newer technique called Positive Psychotherapy. It emphasizes practicing an individual's strengths, instead of focusing on what's wrong.

Pioneering psychologists Martin Seligman, Tayyab Rashid, and Acacia Parks said that Positive Psychotherapy is different from standard interventions for depression by increasing positive emotion, engagement and meaning, rather than directly targeting depressive symptoms. The idea is to focus on and practice what's good about you—your strengths—and not what's bad.

We began with an assessment, a survey of 240 multiple choice questions called the VIA Survey of Character Strengths. It's hosted by the University of Pennsylvania and free to take.

You can find it at

https://www.authentichappiness.sas.upenn.edu/questionnaires/survey-character-strengths#.

The questions are really like statements, such as, "I find the world a very interesting place," or "I always identify the reasons for my actions." It allows you to choose how much you agree or disagree with those statements. The survey collates your answers and ranks you on your character strengths.

The first five traits in my assessment went like this:

Strength #1 - Fairness, equity, and justice

Treating all people fairly is one of your abiding principles. You do not let your personal feelings bias your decisions about other people. You give everyone a chance.

Strength #2 - Creativity, ingenuity, and originality

Thinking of new ways to do things is a crucial part of who you are. You are never content with doing something the conventional way if a better way is possible.

Strength #3 - Bravery and valor

You are a courageous person who does not shrink from threat, challenge, difficulty, or pain. You speak up for what is right even if there is opposition. You act on your convictions.

Strength #4 - Industry, diligence, and perseverance

You work hard to finish what you start. No matter the project, you "get it out the door" in a timely fashion. You do not get distracted when you work, and you take satisfaction in completing tasks.

Strength #5 - Judgment, critical thinking, and open-mindedness

Thinking things through and examining them from all sides are important aspects of who you are. You do not jump to conclusions, and you rely only on solid evidence to make your decisions. You are able to change your mind.

I found the results interesting and somewhat an accurate self-reflection. For several years I'd written an opinion column, called *Frankly Speaking*. It included no-nonsense political and social commentary. I enjoyed doing it, and it truly did reflect my strong feelings for right and wrong, which the assessment ranked as my top strength. Even on Facebook these days, I fight the urge to comment on controversial issues.

In Positive Psychotherapy, the idea is to recognize instances where I exercised my identified strengths and find ways to express these going forward. For example, for me it would be writing an opinion column. That would theoretically make me feel better. Or finding ways to be creative, which writing allows me to do. Or listen to or play music.

I used to enjoy that, although my depression has robbed me of those pleasures.

My therapist and I review my past week's activities to see if we could spot instances of me performing tasks that highlight my strengths. She encourages me to do certain things, like engage more with others, to stimulate my social value strength.

I am finding the Positive Psychotherapy approach to be a bit intangible. But it's early in the process, and I'm going to give it a real chance.

Tidal Wave

Depression is the most prevalent mood disorder in the United States. About one in five Americans experience mental illness in a given year, according to the National Alliance of Mental Illness. Yet only a little more than a third of them seek help.

Major depressive disorder is the leading cause of disability in the U.S. for ages 15 to 44. Half of all chronic mental illness begins by age 14, like in my case, and three-quarters by age 24. Although there is effective treatment, long delays—sometimes decades—pass between the first appearance of symptoms and the time when people get help. Just like me.

Major depressive disorder affects approximately 17.3 million American adults, or about 7.1% of the U.S. population age 18 and older in any given year, according to the National Institute of Mental Health.

According to a 2018 study, the least-educated consistently had the highest rates of moderate to severe depressive symptoms, and the lowest rates of treatment. Disparities in depression by education have persisted or worsened.

Depression affects physical well-being too. For example, those suffering from depression are four times as likely to develop a heart attack as those without a history of the illness. And after a heart attack, they face a significantly higher risk of death or second heart attack.

While environmental circumstances, like a death, a loss, addiction and substance abuse, often lead to mental illness, research has identified neurotransmitters and neural receptors—physiological processes in the brain—as the root cause of many mental illnesses.

In fact, successful drug therapies addressing these chemical deficiencies have worked for many patients seeking relief from mental illness. Doctors have used talk therapies and other more invasive procedures, including electroconvulsive therapy; deep brain stimulation, where an implanted device sends electrical impulses into the brain; and repetitive transcranial magnetic stimulation, where magnetic fields are used to change the activity in certain regions of the brain.

Psychotherapy, also known as talk therapy, is the most common treatment for depression and many other mental illnesses. It's also usually the first line of defense, as it was in my case, against depression. There are plenty of alternatives out there. Talk therapy helped me, but it never got me whole. I've always needed greater intervention.

WHAT IS TREATMENT-RESISTANT DEPRESSION?

In treatment-resistant depression, standard treatments just aren't enough to make a difference. Medications and psychotherapy may not help much at all. Or symptoms could improve yet return repeatedly.

A psychiatrist might look at environmental factors, like life situations that could be triggering the depression. Injuries might have elevated my depression, but it wasn't always true. And it was seldom if ever pointed out by my doctors. There seems to be a disconnect between the physiological and psychological states when addressing health.

Thyroid disorders or heart problems might also be the culprit of the condition, as well as a personality disorder that contributes to the depression. And sometimes, depression might be the wrong diagnosis. You might have bipolar disorder, which requires different treatments, or dysthymia, a milder chronic form of depression.

Medication and counseling strategies are used to address treatment-resistant depression. It's really about trying more things in different ways.

PHARMACEUTICALS

Changing or adding meds, upping doses, and trying off-label medications — ones that are usually prescribed for other conditions— sometimes helps. That worked in my case.

GENETIC TESTING

Some medical professionals also suggest genetic testing through a cytochrome P450 (CYP450) genotyping test. That could indicate how well your body metabolizes a medication, and help a practitioner steer you toward antidepressants that might work best for you. It didn't produce any useful information in my case, but that might not be true for others.

PSYCHOTHERAPY

On the counseling side, you might want to take a different approach. I went from Cognitive Behavior Therapy to Positive Psychotherapy. The jury is still out on that one.

There are other approaches for depression. For example, interpersonal psychotherapy focuses on resolving relationships that might be affecting your depression. Acceptance and commitment therapy, like cognitive behavior therapy and positive psychotherapy, helps you to practice positive behaviors by focusing on mindfulness, reducing avoidant coping styles, and accepting the difficulties that come with life.

Dialectical behavioral therapy teaches you skills to manage painful emotions and decrease conflicts in relationships through mindfulness, building a tolerance to distress, managing emotions, and building effective interpersonal skills.

In psychodynamic treatment, the focus is on understanding and overcoming one's own negative and contradictory feelings and repressed emotions. Like Sigmund Freud's psychoanalysis, it involves a much deeper process of self-examination to improve your interpersonal experiences and relationships. It also teaches you how to analyze and resolve current issues and change behavior based on that understanding.

Of course, there's also marital, family, and group therapies, which involve the participation of others who either have a relationship with you or are also suffering from depression.

PROCEDURES

I've already discussed electroconvulsive therapy (ECT). Although my experience didn't lead to any easing of my depression, it is known to frequently relieve symptoms of major depression. It's an option, and no doubt, is practiced more compassionately than in my case.

Repetitive transcranial magnetic stimulation (rTMS) is another intervention I've mentioned. It's often used when ECT isn't effective. A medical professional places an electromagnetic coil against your scalp near your forehead. An electromagnet creates electric currents that stimulate nerve cells in the region of your brain involved in mood control and depression.

OTHER THINGS TO CONSIDER

Alcohol and recreational drugs might aggravate depression. Both are known to worsen depression, create more environmental issues and make the depression harder to treat.

Stress and a lack of sleep could also contribute to depression. You can reduce or learn to manage stress through exercise, or techniques like yoga, tai chi, meditation, mindfulness and journaling. Exercise used to work for me to an extent, and getting more of it will no doubt lessen my symptoms.

Nature or Nurture

The question lingers. Was I born this way, or did some events in my life make me like this? My depression flared when stressful situations arose. The bully editor. The exposure to tragic events. But why was I reacting this way when others weren't?

A rich body of work exists pointing to genetic factors as the cause of depression and other psychiatric disorders. Depression is known to run in families. Those with major depressive disorder are three times more likely to have a first-degree relative who also has depression.

Studies of twins have shown that about 40 percent of the population was at risk of depression due to genetics.

But a 2017 study published in the Journal of the American Medical Association Psychiatry reported that the environment you were raised in has just as much influence as genetics over your risk factors from getting major depression.

The results were based on a population of 2.2 million subjects in Sweden, along with their parents. The study found that genetic factors and household environment contributed equally to the odds that the illness would be transmitted from parents to children. It discredited previous findings that genetic predisposition plays a larger role in inheriting depression.

The results have a number of implications for research and treatment. While some have searched for the "mental illness gene," some researchers believe that psycho-social factors should be looked at more closely.

Other researchers suggest that a promising avenue for preventing and treating depression lies in uncovering both the genetic and environmental determinants of the disorder as well as its interaction.

Environmental risk factors for depression include poverty, negative family relationships and parental divorce, child maltreatment, and other stressful life events. Researchers wrote that while the risk of depression is higher immediately after experiencing these environmental difficulties, the effects of adversity can last over a lifetime.

Right now, it looks as though there are a number of possible causes of depression. Some people have a genetic predisposition to depression, which can then be triggered by a stressful situation in life. Others suffer from challenging upbringings that make depression more likely. It's a complicated disease awaiting major breakthroughs.

NATURAL REMEDIES VERSUS MEDS

We have a friend with a college-aged child who struggles with depression. The friend decided to treat the child holistically at an inpatient center. The child doesn't take any psychopharmaceutical medications.

The treatment helped and seemed to put them on a better track, although I am told the child still suffers from anxiety and depression. This reignited a debate with my wife about psych meds. I take a lot of them, and some have side effects, like lethargy and increased appetite.

My wife doesn't believe in the psych meds I'm taking. She thinks the meds are poisoning my system and the side effects aren't worth it. She believes in vitamins, herbs, nutrition, exercise and personal responsibility. She thinks our medical establishment is just in the business of profiting off the pharmaceuticals I'm prescribed.

I, of course, have a different point of view. I know my depression ballooned when I tried getting off one medication, and benefited greatly when I tried a new one.

Talk therapy has helped me, but never got me to a really good place. It gave me some tools to cope with anxiety and depression. But after years of talk therapy, with different therapists, it all begins to sound the same.

My wife takes medications for a couple of common ailments. Yet, she doesn't equate that to treating mental illness. It's a bias even she, who has lived with a depressed person for so many years, still internalizes. Somehow, in her mind, mental illness is not a medical disease like rheumatoid arthritis.

I know first-hand the effects of medication on my depression. She is convinced I'm doped up on unnecessary meds that could be replaced with meditation and some over-the-counter vitamins. I would probably benefit from her support of my choices.

FIGHTING THE BUREAUCRACY

A friend of mine suggested that I get a copy of my psychiatric records. It would help me remember episodes I couldn't and give me additional insight into my condition. I requested my records from the practice I was going to, a large health system provider in Lehigh Valley, Pa. Much to my surprise, I was told I would need permission to get those records.

A few days later, I received a phone call from the psychiatrist's office. My request for my records was denied. No reason was given. I was stunned. You would think your own medical records would be available to you, that you had a right to have them.

I looked up the law. It's under the federal guidelines of HIPAA (Health Insurance Portability and Accountability Act of 1996). That's the law that provides data privacy and security provisions for safeguarding medical information.

According to the law, I was entitled to my records. But there was a hitch, a special provision for psychiatric records. Those records could be withheld from a patient if the doctor believes it could pose a danger to the patient or someone else.

It was ridiculous. Those records were all based on my own outpourings in sessions with the psychiatrists. I'd been stable for a few years, with my depression under relative control. How could it now lead me to harm myself or others?

I was told the head psychiatrist at the practice was reluctant to release the information because she didn't really know me. So why not get to know me? Read the file. Speak to my current doctor, or the one I had seen for years before then.

It seemed that little attempt was made to determine my fitness for this information. I felt the medical care institution could be covering itself from potential litigation or liability should I someday hurt someone or myself.

I was told there was an appeal process, but that appeal would go through doctors at the same health system. So those people would have the same corporate responsibilities and liabilities. The system was stacked against the patient.

I spoke to the medical director of the facility, a clinician turned administrator. He suggested I narrow my request and ask for psychiatric evaluations only. That request would have a better chance of succeeding than trying to get my complete set of records.

I finally received the official denial in the mail with a form to request an appeal, which I immediately filled out. This time I asked only for my psychiatric records. The response brought many surprises.

THE RECORDS ARRIVE

I finally received some of my medical records from my psychiatrist's office during the fall of 2019.

My initial request was denied—the doctors feared my reading these would do more harm than good. I questioned the denial and asked for an appeal.

The director of the psychiatric practice explained the mountains of notes could stir up bad memories and put me in a worse place than I already was. He wasn't terribly convincing, and having looked over the records himself, didn't think it would do much harm. He suggested I request my psych evaluations, something I was more likely to be granted.

What sealed the deal was a conversation with my own psychiatrist. She truly believed that reviewing the records could set me back. I trusted her. I accepted the decision and awaited the psych evaluations.

What I received was a rather small package chock-full of test results, one- or two-word evaluations of standard categories, and prescription records. What was missing was any significant narrative of my condition.

My diagnosis stood out to me: Major depressive disorder, recurrent, chronic, severe, without psychotic features.

It was the first time I focused on the term major depressive disorder. Yet I was grateful I wasn't diagnosed with psychotic features, though I wondered what those could be.

PSYCHOTIC FEATURES

Major depression with psychotic features is where a person with depression loses touch with reality. The condition causes people to hallucinate — see, hear or believe things that aren't real. About 20 percent of patients with major depression suffer from psychosis.

The hallucinations come in two varieties. In one, mood-congruent psychotic features, the content of the hallucinations and delusions is consistent with typical depressive themes. Those include feelings of personal inadequacy, guilt or worthlessness.

With mood-incongruent psychotic features, the hallucinations and delusions don't involve the typical depressive themes. Symptoms are inconsistent with the dominant mood.

Symptoms may include:

- Persecutory delusions (thinking you are being persecuted).
- Thought insertion — the feeling that thoughts are not your own, but rather belong to someone else and have been inserted into your mind.
- Thought broadcasting, where there is a belief that others can hear or are aware of an individual's thoughts.

- Delusions of control — the belief that another person, group of people, or external force controls your thoughts, feelings, impulses, or behavior.

The symptoms of both mood-congruent psychotic features and mood-incongruent psychotic features can be dangerous and frightening for the patient. It can also increase the risk of suicide. Prompt diagnosis and treatment may prevent someone from hurting themselves or others.

REASSURANCE AND *BAD THOUGHTS*

There were other encouraging notations in my evaluations besides not being psychotic. I didn't have suicidal ideations. I did, as I've recounted, but I always kept those to myself to prevent my psychiatrist from putting it in my records. I knew life insurance companies had access to those records, and it would affect my premiums. Always thinking.

In fact, I had a code word for expressing suicidal thoughts to my psychiatrists. I always called it "bad thoughts." As in, "I was beginning to have some bad thoughts." I thought they'd pick up on it. Apparently, they didn't.

The records indicated I had stable housing and employment, income, insurance, benefits and positive family support, along with children and pets.

One recurrent question of all my various physician visits was whether there were guns in the home—there weren't any. And thank God for that. Who knows what might have happened if I had easy access to a firearm during my darkest times, when the demons were knocking on the door?

Then there were lab results on abused drugs. Ethanol (alcohol), negative; methamphetamine (AKA meth), negative. Cocaine, cannabinoids, MDMA, methadone, barbiturates, phencyclidine (a synthetic hallucinogenic), amphetamines, all negative. I was proud.

Then it got to oxycodone. The results were positive. Even though it was prescribed by a doctor for my back, I felt my record was blemished. I also tested positive for benzodiazepine, the anti-anxiety drug my psychiatrist prescribed me.

All in all, the record indicated no illicit drug or excessive alcohol use.

According to the reports, I had a longstanding history of depression dating back to 1991, when I first sought help. My most prominent symptoms were decreased energy and concentration. I would have thought it would have been dark moods.

SSRIs

The psychiatrist indicated I was on too high a dose of a selective serotonin reuptake inhibitors (SSRIs). SSRIs are the most commonly prescribed type of antidepressants.

The compound treats depression by increasing levels of serotonin in the brain. Serotonin is a neurotransmitter, a chemical messenger carrying signals between brain nerve cells, or neurons. It is believed to have an impact on depression.

SSRIs block serotonin reabsorption into neurons. That makes more serotonin available to improve transmission of messages between neurons. Common brands include Citalopram (Celexa), Escitalopram (Lexapro), Fluoxetine (Prozac), Paroxetine (Paxil, Pexeva) and Sertraline (Zoloft).

I've tried them all with varying degrees of success and side effects. The side effects can be nasty, like nausea, drowsiness, nervousness, agitation and reduced libido. I had to try several to find one that had the fewest side effects. In my case, that was Lexapro. The report indicated the doctor talked to me about serotonin syndrome, which I don't doubt but can't remember.

Serotonin syndrome symptoms include:[3]

- Agitation or restlessness
- Confusion
- Rapid heart rate and high blood pressure
- Dilated pupils
- Loss of muscle coordination or twitching muscles
- Muscle rigidity
- Heavy sweating

---

[3] Mayo Clinic, Serotonin syndrome, https://www.mayoclinic.org/diseases-conditions/serotonin-syndrome/symptoms-causes/syc-20354758

- Diarrhea
- Headache
- Shivering
- Goosebumps

If not treated, severe serotonin syndrome can be fatal.

I do have elevated blood pressure levels. But I can't recall having many of those other conditions, although history has shown I have a high tolerance to medications and a poor recall of events.

DIAGNOSES

Along with the severe major depression, my problem list as of August 2018 included generalized anxiety disorder, post-traumatic stress disorder (from the Christmas massacre), hyperlipidemia (too many fat cells in the blood—thanks a lot), essential hypertension (high blood pressure without a known secondary cause), obstructive sleep apnea, spinal stenosis and back ache. No surprises there. Reading that didn't have a detrimental effect on my psychological well-being. It was like looking at the ingredients on a can of tuna.

My family medical history was sketchy, since both of my parents died decades ago. And there's my faulty memory to consider. Diabetes, heart disease, stroke, and a couple of cancers were the only ones I could remember. Motor skills and thinking questioned

In the back of the packet was a two-page evaluation issued in May of 2010 by my previous psychiatrist. In it, she noted I exhibited psychomotor retardation.

Psychomotor retardation is a slowing down of thought and a reduction of physical movements caused by an underlying psychiatric disorder—mainly depression. It can cause a visible slowing of physical and emotional reactions, including speech and affect.

That was news to me.

An affected person's speech may include long pauses or losing one's train of thought. Also common are delayed responsiveness and difficulty following another person's conversation. It takes longer to do complex mental processes, like simple calculations or mapping out directions.

That just didn't seem to fit me, although it was right there in black and white. I guess if the onset was gradual, I might not have noticed it.

Other symptoms include:[4]

- Sluggishness when walking or changing positions, such as getting up from a chair
- Slumped posture
- Speaking in a soft, monotonous voice
- Staring into space and reduced eye contact

---

[4] Psychomotor Retardation in Bipolar Disorder, Verywell Mind, 2019

- Diminished facility with fine motor tasks, such as writing, using scissors, and tying shoelaces
- Impaired ability to perform tasks requiring eye-hand coordination, such as catching a ball, shaving, and applying makeup
- Slow reaction time, such as when reaching for a falling object

These symptoms were familiar, and when asked, my wife agreed. She reminded me of it constantly. She blamed it on the side effects of the drugs I was taking. I blamed it on a bad back. Turns out, she was partially right.

Many of the medications I was taking had known side effects similar to those described by psychomotor retardation. It's hard to know if it's the depression or the drugs. But my instinct is to go with the diagnosis of my doctor. My allegiance to my doctor's explanations is a fault of mine my wife continually reminds me of.

DYSPHORIA

The evaluation described my mood as dysphoric. That's a sadness, heaviness, numbness, or sometimes irritability and mood swings, a loss of interest or pleasure in my usual activities, difficulty concentrating, or loss of energy and motivation.

That diagnosis was right on. Nothing that used to give me pleasure still did, like music, sporting events, exercise or getting together with friends.

The report also described my mood as angry and anxious. Both qualities are still a part of my symptomatology.

Another entry said my associations are occasionally loose. That's a thought disorder where my responses did not relate to the interviewer's questions, or one paragraph, sentence, or phrase was not logically connected to those that occur before or after.

That was surprising. I always thought of myself as direct and focused. It was disappointing to read this. My more recent evaluation mentioned this characteristic too. I need to be more aware of my responses in the future, especially since I work in a professional setting, where communication is key.

All in all, the content of my psychological evaluations was disappointing. It didn't provide me with significant insight into my condition or trigger memories of events that would help me understand my disease. It was more descriptive than interpretive, and just wasn't helpful. I may lobby for the full medical history in the future.

RESISTANCE

Most of those with depression find relief through medications, talk therapies, more exotic treatments like electroconvulsive therapy or any combination of the above.

My depression has been labeled treatment resistant depression (TRD). Symptoms can range from mild to severe and could require experimenting with a number of treatments to identify what helps.

That's been my journey. From medication to medication, various talk therapy counselors and ECT. Most have been unsuccessful.

TRD is where a patient hasn't responded to proper doses of two different antidepressants, taken for a sufficient duration of time, which is usually six weeks.

Ha. Try 30 years. That's been my journey.

It's an unsatisfying situation. I've been willing to try new things, yet few have proved helpful. It involves experimenting with various medications at various dosages, with weeks and months in between to determine if it's helping.

Then of course you can add or layer medications, try those at various levels, and wait weeks or months to see if that works. It's a trial-and-error process. I've been through that for years. And although antidepressants may not cure depression, they can reduce symptoms.

I've taken medications for other types of diagnoses, like schizophrenia, just to see if it worked. I've even gone through genetic testing, which is supposed to guide the psychiatrist in what medications are most likely to be helpful. That was a bust – it only confirmed what the doctor already knew from years of trial and error. An expensive one too, since my insurance wouldn't cover the entire cost of the testing.

Psychological counseling has had a moderate impact on my moods. I've tried five different therapists, and I clicked with some more than others.

But I'm not giving up. I saw a new therapist for counseling about a year ago, but I knew it wasn't going to work out after a few weeks. The therapist was nearing retirement age, and was just mailing it in. He strained to figure out what to talk to me about. I wasn't gaining any insight or learning any new tools.

There's another treatment I just became aware of, called vagus nerve stimulation (VNS)[5]. VNS is only used after other brain stimulation therapies such as ECT and repetitive transcranial magnetic stimulation have not improved symptoms.

VNS stimulates the vagus nerve with electrical impulses through an implanted device. Electrical signals travel along the nerve to the mood centers of the brain, hopefully improving symptoms of depression. The vagus nerve travels from the brain through the face and thorax to the abdomen.

With my track record, there's no way I'm going for an implant of a device that may or may not work.

I follow other guidelines — I don't drink or do drugs. I get regular exercise. I try new therapies, drugs and otherwise. Yet my depression is still there.

---

[5] Vagus Nerve Stimulation, American Association of Neurological Surgeons, 2020 https://www.aans.org/en/Patients/Neurosurgical-Conditions-and-Treatments/Vagus-Nerve-Stimulation

According to a story written on behalf of healthcare provider Johnson and Johnson[6], women and senior citizens experience TRD at higher rates. Those who experience severe or frequent periods of depression are also more likely to suffer from TRD. And someone afflicted with another illness is also more likely to be diagnosed with TRD. It's an unfortunate diagnosis, but the destructiveness of depression motivates me to continue to seek relief.

NO LACK OF WILLPOWER

At 63, Robin Williams seemed to have it all. A brilliant, unique talent. An incomparable body of work. The respect of his peers. A family. Job opportunities. Yet, somehow, it wasn't enough.

In 2014, like many celebrities since, he chose to end his life. The question, of course, is not what, but why. And the answer lies in this murky corner of medicine we treat with whispers, the way we dealt with AIDS in the 1980s. Williams was said to have had major depression. It's a mental illness, yet it's met with hushes and shame among those who have it.

Depression is a disease of the brain. Like many diseases, it produces pain. So much pain that some take their lives to make it stop. What kind of pain could drive someone to do that?

---

[6] 4 Things We Now Know About Treatment-Resistant Depression, Jessica Brown, Johnson and Johnson, https://www.jnj.com/health-and-wellness/4-facts-about-treatment-resistant-depression

The pain from depression is like the grief of first learning you've lost someone close to you. There's shock, horror, confusion and inconsolable sadness.

Now, imagine waking up with that grief every morning as if it were fresh news. Then imagine reliving the news all day. Go to sleep, and it's Groundhog Day.

Those who take their lives don't want to hurt themselves—they just want to end their suffering.

Doctors say deep depression, along with suicidal thoughts, ease with time, and that the suicidal period passes. That's why they call suicide *a permanent solution to a temporary problem*. The trick is to seek help when you think you might be afflicted. There are so many interventions and resources to get you through that critical *darkest moment* period. But you have to ask.

Yet herein is the Catch-22. There's an entire generation of Baby Boomers, like myself, who consider the disease nothing more than *a lack of willpower*. That kind of destructive attitude discourages people from seeking the help they need.

In fact, we sometimes react to suicide with anger, as in "How could they be so selfish?" Never, "How could they have been so sick, and we never noticed it?"

I never met Robin Williams. I saw him jogging alone in Central Park once, dressed in heavy layers, a scarf, hat and gloves.

He looked just like the rest of us that winter day, struggling to put one foot in front of the other, and withstand the cold. And despite his extraordinary gifts, he died of a treatable disease that will take more lives until we change our attitudes toward depression and its treatment.

Poor Robin Williams. He lived such an extraordinary life and died in such an unnecessary way.

If you are having thoughts of suicide, call the National Suicide Prevention Lifeline at 1-800-273-8255 (TALK). You can find a list of additional resources at SpeakingOfSuicide.com/resources.

EMPATHY FAILS

After years of having my back, driving me to ETCs and putting up with my moods, my wife recently told me she'd thrown in the towel. She no longer cared about my depressive symptoms. She said the empathy train had left the station a long time ago. That shook me. She lost her compassion for the daily struggles I faced.

On the one hand, I understood it. I put her and my son through hell. But on the other hand, if we are to believe that mental illness is no different than any other type of medical condition, would we abandon our empathy for someone who had another chronic illness?

I doubt it. It's another manifestation of the stigma, that mental illness equals mental weakness. It makes me sadder that it came from my wife. She should know better.

What it means to me is she no longer supports my battles with pain, sadness and grief.

She once told me she read that people don't want to hear about other people's depression. After that, I spoke to her a lot less about it. Practically not at all. It's a shame because most people with depression seek support and someone to talk to.

I'm relegated to the therapist I pay to listen to me. That will have to do. I've only told a couple of people that I suffer from depression and am afraid that talking about it would make others uncomfortable.

But it's hard for someone close to you to say, "Your illness isn't real, and you're not helping yourself enough. I'm not having any of it."

SIGNS OF RECOVERY

A Small Success

Both my psychiatrist and I were frustrated by the lack of progress I was making. My depression persisted and I was despondent. I had been seeing that psychiatrist for a number of years and I truly felt that she became invested in my success. She once told me psychiatrists were different types of doctors because they genuinely cared about their patients in a deeper sense.

The psychiatrist suggested adding another pill to my daily regimen. It was called Rexulti—also known as Brexpiprazole. Brexpiprazole is described as a second-generation antipsychotic or atypical antipsychotic. It is simply a newer form of antipsychotic with fewer side effects. Brexpiprazole is said to rebalance dopamine and serotonin to improve thinking, mood and behavior. It's also used to treat schizophrenics.

When presented with new drug alternatives, I always asked if it would cause weight gain. That was a game-changer for me. I am a big guy and didn't need to put on any weight.

But again, I was in immediate need. So, I dropped my pretenses and agreed to take it as an add-on to my daily drug dosages.

I felt the effects almost immediately—within three or four days. That's immediate in the sluggishly long timetable of psychiatric medication responses.

My severe depression became more moderate. It gave me a huge feeling of relief. I wasn't cured, but the edge it took off my symptoms was remarkable. I felt I had found an answer. Of course, there were side effects. The worst was weight gain. I put on about 20 pounds in a short amount of time. Along with the increased appetite came fatigue and some agitation, all known side effects of the drug. But it was a small trade-off to feeling better.

When I reported the results of the new medication to my psychiatrist, I described my mood as like "night and day." She was thrilled. I could tell she was not just happy for me but pleased that as a professional, she'd found something that would help me. It had been a long road for both of us.

My depression later became a little deeper, probably triggered by a toxic work environment. The doctor increased the dosage of the Rexulti to the maximum. It had the unfortunate effect of numbing me to my environment, unable to feel much of anything.

This was a problem for a writer who has to tap into their creative side. It also left me acting socially isolated. I eventually went down in dosage to the original amount I had been prescribed.

Seeking relief from depression isn't about making yourself happy. It's about getting rid of the sadness.

I still take the medication. It helped stabilize my moods. Not cure my depression, mind you. But it's allowed me to work without being torn apart everyday with depressive thoughts and feelings.

AN UNEXPECTED TURN

Ahh, the vacuum cleaner. It's Black Death to me. Searing pain. So is shoveling, sweeping and anything that forces me to lean forward. Even after successful back surgery to correct disc and nerve problems, my lower back pain reappeared. Always there, it changed my normally unremarkable expression to a grimace. The combination of movement and the inflexible spinal joints from compressed discs created a constant burning ache.

My orthopedic doctor gave me a list of five alternative treatments, from physical therapy and spinal injections to medications. I've tried them all, yet the pain got worse.

I elected to go with the fifth and most extreme choice—lumbar spinal fusion. It's where a surgeon joins or fuses two or more levels of spinal vertebrae to stabilize the normally semi-flexible joints that allow you to bend and twist.

They use rods and screws to fuse the vertebrae, in my case three levels, and add bone grafts. My own bone would eventually grow over that structure, solidify, and provide better stability between the fused joints. We set the date for Oct. 9, 2019.

I got my ducks in a row. I helped to put away the summer furniture and cleaned shirts that I could wear over a brace. I scheduled my work interviews at my new job with a scientific instruments company for a time during recovery when I thought I'd be able to function.

The hospital was about 90 miles from my home. Not conducive to family or friendly visits, but who wants company when you look like crap anyway.

Then, two nights before the surgery, it hit the national news. My hospital was transferring all extreme premature babies out of the facility. Bacterially contaminated equipment infected several of them in the past few months and killed three. Poor babies. And their families. I had one more thing to worry about.

The surgeon suggested I read about the procedure beforehand. I was concerned. It sounded like a long, challenging recovery. And the idea of having my spine bound with metal rods was a little freaky. But the pain won me over. I had little choice. Do it then and have a few pain-free years ahead or wait for it to get worse. I wanted to enjoy my time now.

My wife and I got up in the middle of the night to make the drive to the hospital. We arrived at 6 a.m. She gave me a hug at the car, left me at the front doors and headed home. No sense in her waiting around for hours just to talk to the surgeon since she could do that by phone.

And it wasn't my first dance. There was the other back surgery, two knees, my shoulders, nose and whatever else I can't remember. I'd be fine there alone, high on pain medication, watching CNN.

It took two hours of processing until I got to the operating room. Whatever pill they gave me to relax wasn't working. I was wide awake, aware of every stainless-steel cabinet and bright light in that room.

The anesthesiologist, who I met an hour earlier, injected something into my IV. "You'll be asleep in a few seconds," he said.

I stared at the bright overhead lights, waiting for the juice to hit me. But nothing happened.

"In 10 seconds, you'll be asleep," he said.

Again, the time passed. I stared, counting in my head, and again, nothing happened. It was beginning to get uncomfortable in there.

"Any second now," the anesthesiologist said nervously.

In a few more moments, I was out.

I awoke in a bright, noisy recovery area, alongside more than a dozen other patients. A nurse, I assume, reassured me I was out of surgery. I was uncomfortable, but not in pain.

Through the haze of heavy narcotics, I could see three corrections officers loitering in the aisle between the two rows of hospital beds. Across from me was an inmate, and the COs were standing watch over him. Another inmate occupied a space a few yards down, curiously wearing his prison oranges. There were several correctional facilities nearby.

My bed was in a tiny cubicle of a space, made smaller by a structural pillar that took up most of the area. They couldn't even fit a rolling table next to me. But it was temporary, I told myself, until they got me to a room.

Meanwhile, the bedded inmate across from me had a huge, curtained space. Several family members were sitting in chairs around his bed. Bonus visitation time. I was alone and could barely fit an IV around mine. With his curtains closed, it looked like a princely harem tent in the desert. It just didn't seem fair.

In the interim, the pain crept up, and from time to time I'd ask for more medicine, which I got. But the minutes turned into hours, and hours into nighttime. They didn't have a bed for me on the orthopedics floor, where they insisted, I be brought.

So, I spent the night in the bright, noisy recovery area. Someone eventually moved my bed to a quieter cubicle farther from the nursing station. It even had a TV on a swivel, which was hard to enjoy at the time.

I spent a peaceful night in that space, if you consider being awakened for dress changes and blood pressure checks peaceful.

The way the medical staff dispensed pain meds changed since my last back surgery just three years earlier. They were more conservative, waiting for me to ask for it. And they quickly weaned me off the IV pain meds to less powerful pills. Times had changed.

They moved me to a private room the next morning. It was sharp. Blonde wooden floors and a huge window overlooked rolling green Pennsylvania hills.

Technicians fitted me for a back brace and returned with it the next day. It was an enormous, hard plastic corset that Velcroed at the waist, encased my midsection, went up my back and extended over my butt. All I could think of was how in the world I would be able to wear work clothing over it without looking like Frankenstein. The technician told me I'd have to wear it for three months.

"Adapt," he said.

I was hospitalized for four days. The worst part was removing the dressing over the incision during periodic changes. The surgeon warned me that the skin on the lower back was ultra-sensitive, and it would be painful. When they took off the fluid-soaked bandage, the adhesive tape felt like it was ripping the skin from the already raw surface of my back.

I was cautious when I got home. I wore the brace, didn't lift anything heavy and moved slowly. No twisting or bending. I got slip-on shoes for the recovery, and those babies came in handy.

A health professional paid me a visit a couple of days later. She gave me this device that looked like an old flip phone with wires attached to it. Those wires went to adhesive electrodes that stuck on my back.

The device was a bone growth stimulator. It sent signals to the bone grafts in my spine to encourage solid bone to form. I'd have to reposition the electrodes every day along the eight-inch incision and wear it for 10 months. They didn't tell me about that one beforehand. Good thing.

After about a week, I no longer needed pain medication, including Tylenol. My initial recovery was quick, although the back was sore. But nothing compared to the pain I had before.

My wife began to notice my constant scowl disappeared. My mood lifted. The feelings of sadness subsided. I wasn't happy—I just wasn't sad. The depression eased.

My psychiatrist later reminded me that pain caused stress, which in turn often contributed to depression. The lifting of that stress, she suggested, may have softened some of my depressive symptoms.

It has only been a few months, but there's no question my depression is milder than before. Although I knew through my research this was possible, I hadn't related to it. I hope it continues.

GETTING HELP

I was lucky. I had a loved one who led me down the road to treatment for my depression. The truth is, Teresa demanded it—get help or she'd leave. Others aren't so lucky. Yet there are still alternatives.

The National Suicide Prevention Lifeline, at 800-273-8255 (TALK) is available 24 hours a day. You won't simply be told not to hurt yourself. It provides confidential support, local resources and coping strategies to carry you through your immediate crisis. The lifeline is a national network of local crisis centers that provides free support to people in suicidal crisis or emotional distress.

There are support groups throughout the U.S. The National Alliance on Mental Illness also has a hotline number—800-950-NAMI—that can hook you up to one of those groups.

Seeking treatment changed my life from a constant pool of negativity and pain to a functional level, where I could enjoy certain things in life. I could make plans and dream, rather than exist in a murky soup of demons whispering in my ears.

The depression remains, and there are certainly triggers that make it worse. But I'm more aware of those triggers and have added tools to handle it when it arises.

My chronic pain has backed off, providing me with emotional relief, and my meds, which have remained the same for a while, seem to be helping. It took a long time to get here, but the alternative was the unthinkable.

In the winter of 2020, during the Covid-19 outbreak, I was diagnosed with prostate cancer. I accepted the news with little emotion. Getting the news was nothing compared to the pain of battling the monsters that plagued my soul for all these years.

I don't fear death — I fear living.

HOPE

It's been a long journey, and I reflect on it from time to time. Some things are apparent to me.

Buzz Aldrin was the second man to walk on the moon. He also has severe depression. So have actors Christian Bale, Johnny Depp and Brad Pitt at some point. Add to that list Barbara Bush, Ellen DeGeneres and Mozart. Iconic musicians like the late Ray Charles, Bruce Springsteen, Paul McCartney and Eminem. Beyoncé, for God's sake. Abraham Lincoln. The great Hulk Hogan. Even Hall of Fame quarterback and sports host Terry Bradshaw, the happy-go-lucky, bigger than life personality. And that's but a tiny sampling of celebrities who experienced what Winston Churchill called *the black dog*. Oh, he suffered. It's more common than you think.

Yet all these people overcame their battle with this illness to accomplish great things.

I have learned much during my journey through depression. It's been the toughest struggle I've ever fought, and I know it's ongoing. Like an alcoholic, I'll probably always carry this illness. But I learned I can treat it.

I won't say, "I'm feeling better—I don't need my meds anymore." That's a trap that leads to a cycle of emotional dips and crashes.

So, as I experience this easing of symptoms, I refuse to be fooled into complacency, thinking some of the underlying factors don't still exist. The back pain may have quieted, but my upbringing and brain chemistry keeps me at risk. Nurture and nature can't be ignored.

I've had some successes and built some good relationships. I could do better. I'll continue to see a psychologist for talk therapy and try to remember the lessons learned through cognitive and positive therapies—doing a reality check on what I believe to be true and exercise my strengths. I will still see a psychiatrist for psych meds. I'll let her guide me if I'm considering changes.

Despite the overwhelming sadness depression can bring, I think each of us can address this disease, to some degree, and improve our lives. Treatment has always given me hope. And while treatment has disappointed me more than not, I will continue to seek its rewards. The results are worth it.

Research into depression goes on. We are still in the infancy of understanding mental illness. I'll continue to read about new therapies, and when treatments are shown to be effective, I will consider them.

After all, Lincoln fought through his depression to unite a splintered country. Mozart composed music still revered centuries later. And Buzz Aldrin—heck, he walked on the moon. Yet they fought the demons. So, there's no reason why I can't do better in my own life. I believe that.

I'm glad I survived my thoughts of suicide. I would have missed the joys of my son's high school and college graduations. Plus, his successes along the way. And all the things yet to come.

About The Author

Howard Frank

Howard Frank is an award-winning journalist and author of two books, Talk to the Devil and The Colors of the Rainbow – A Children's Guide to Spectroscopy. A native New Yorker who lived on the Upper West Side of Manhattan for most of his professional life, Howard worked in licensing and marketing in the fashion industry.

In the aftermath of an IPO of the company's stock, Howard chose to pursue a career in writing. He joined the staff of Gannett's Pocono Record, a daily newspaper. There he won numerous awards for beat and investigative stories. He wrote a weekly opinion column called Frankly Speaking that drew a large following and won him an Associated Press award.

After a dozen years at the paper, he transitioned to content writing, traveling the country and documenting researchers' scientific journeys of discovery in a variety of fields such as nanotechnology and extraterrestrial life.

Today, he is at home in the mountains of Northeast Pennsylvania, where the closeness of nature provides more than ample inspiration for his writing.